F-86 SABRE
VS
MiG-15

Korea 1950–53

DOUGLAS C. DILDY & WARREN E. THOMPSON

First published in Great Britain in 2013 by Osprey Publishing,
PO Box 883, Oxford, OX1 9PL, UK
1385 Broadway, 5th Floor, New York, NY 10018, USA
Email: info@ospreypublishing.com

Osprey Publishing is part of Bloomsbury Publishing Plc

A CIP catalogue record for this book is available from the British Library

ISBN: 978 1 78096 319 8
PDF eBook ISBN: 978 1 78096 320 4
ePub ISBN: 978 1 78096 321 1

Edited by Tony Holmes
Cover artworks and battlescene by Wiek Luijken
Three-views, cockpits, gunsight and armament scrap views by Jim Laurier
Index by Alan Thatcher
Originated by PDQ Digital Media Solutions, UK
Printed in China through World Print Ltd.

17 18 19 20 21   12 11 10 9 8 7 6 5 4 3

Osprey Publishing is supporting the Woodland Trust, the UK's leading
woodland conservation charity, by funding the dedication of trees.

www.ospreypublishing.com

Authors' Acknowledgement
Like the design and development of a great airplane, composing a comparative
history such as this book is not the product of just one or two people.
The authors gratefully appreciate the generous contributions of the following
individuals: F-86 historians Larry Davis (US) and Duncan Curtis (UK) for their
technical information and corrections, and many F-86 photographs. Richard
Keener and the late George Jones for their valuable insights into the USAF jet
training regimen and F-86 combat operations, respectively. David McClaren for
is meticulous research and comprehensive accounting of F-86 losses in Korea.
National Museum of the USAF archivist Brett Stolle for his exhaustive MiG-15
technical research. Editor Tim Callaway and artist Zaur Eylanbekov for the use
of their MiG-15 photographs. Air War College professor Xiaoming Zhang for
providing substantial information on the People's Liberation Army Air Force's
experience with the MiG-15, and for his excellent feedback on the manuscript
as a whole. Korean War historian Robert F. Dorr and Vietnam historian
W. Howard Plunkett for their thorough reviews and instructive critiques.

F-86 Sabre cover art
On November 2, 1951, after ten months of duelling over the Yalu River, Lt Col
George L. Jones, the deputy commander of the 4th FIG, led 12 F-86As from the
334th FIS "Fighting Eagles" covering two formations of F-84E fighter-bombers
attacking rail yards and supply dumps near the river. As the second group of
Thunderjets began their egress from the target area, 16 MiG-15s from the 303rd
IAD intercepted the departing fighter-bombers. Jones and his wingman, 1Lt
Richard Pincoski, attacked the leading MiG, resulting in an extended engagement
in which both USAF fighters expended all of their 0.50-cal ammunition. "I knew
I was riding a tiger, a Russian 'Honcho'", Lt Col Jones later recalled. "I told 'Red 2'
that I was not going to let him get away, and to move out of my way. I flashed
by my wingman, and with all the holes and metal fragments sticking out of the
MiG's wing and fuselage, he had picked up a lot of drag, causing his airspeed to
slow considerably. I figured that my overtake speed was in excess of 100 knots.
The MiG pilot was watching my closure rate, and to avoid me he pushed over
into a steep dive. Instantly, his fighter snap-rolled to the left. That did it!
Evidently, the damaged airframe could not take the stress and something broke.
'Red 2' called out that the pilot had bailed out. I watched the empty MiG go
straight down into the ground 15,000ft below me." (Artwork by Wiek Luijken)

MiG-15 cover art
At 1116 hrs on July 29, 1951, the 176th GvIAP launched 16 MiG-15bis from
Langtao airfield to cover the disengagement of the 303rd IAD's 17th IAP.
Leading his *zveno* (four-aircraft formation) up to nearly 46,000ft, Guards Capt
Sergei "Baida" Kramarenko covered the "strike flight", led by the regimental
commander, Guards Lt Col Sergey Yishnyakov. Approaching Chongju, the
MiGs were met by eight F-86As from the 4th FIG's 335th FIS. Kramarenko
warned his commander and led his formation down approximately 13,000ft
against the enemy's trailing four-ship. He later recalled, "Two Sabres went to left
and two to the right, and I went towards the right [pair]. The Sabres began to
dive, but by then the range had decreased, and at about 400m I opened fire.
I saw hits all over the Sabre leader, which, trailing smoke, kept on diving.
My wingman jumped the second Sabre, but his aircraft began to shake due to its
speed having almost reached 1,000km/h, and consequently he missed. When we
pulled out of the dive we saw that only one Sabre remained below us – there was
no trace of the second. Soon the ground control confirmed that he had crashed."
F-86A-5 49-1098 was severely damaged by both 23mm and 37mm cannon hits
on the engine, rudder, and elevators, and it went into a left-hand spiraling dive,
smoking badly. Escorted by his three squadronmates, the pilot flew the disabled
jet to a point six miles north of Suwon AB, where he ejected safely. This was
Kramarenko's fifth kill of the Korean War, making him the first Soviet ace
whose victories were scored exclusively against enemy jet fighters. (Artwork
by Wiek Luijken)

CONTENTS

INTRODUCTION

The history of the Korean War is actually the story of two conflicts. On the national level it was a war between two halves of one people, arbitrarily separated by powers much greater than themselves, fighting for the reunification of their land – hence the northern Democratic People's Republic of Korea's (DPRK) invasion of the southern Republic of Korea (ROK) beginning June 25, 1950.

At the regional level it was a campaign between the US-led coalition of western democracies fighting under the banner of the United Nations (UN) and the Communist partnership of the USSR and the newly-formed (in December 1949) People's Republic of China (PRC). Once the DPRK's Korean People's Army (KPA) was forcibly ejected from South Korea by UN Command (UNC) forces, the PRC became primarily responsible for their side's ground operations, while the USSR – because the PRC's neophyte air force was not yet prepared for combat – provided air cover.

This contest, pitting three Communist countries against the US-led UNC, was fought – bitterly, but with limited local objectives by both sides – within the global context of the Cold War, an ideological struggle that was just getting into its stride following the Berlin Crisis, the formation of NATO and the utter defeat of the Chinese Nationalist Kuomintang (KMT) during the previous two years.

From the time that the North Korean People's Air Force (KPAF) had been swept from the skies, the US's Far East Air Forces (FEAF, pronounced like "leaf", and later retitled the Pacific Air Forces or PACAF) maintained almost absolute air supremacy over the front. Behind the Communist lines, however, the issue was not so clearly decided – at least not at that time. This northwest corner of North Korea between the Chongchon River and the Yalu, from the shores of Korea Bay to the central highlands, was the arena for an aerial contest unique in the annals of air warfare.

Within this volume of airspace (from the surface to almost 50,000ft (15,240m)), especially at the upper reaches of it, for two-and-a-half years a battle raged almost exclusively between two specific antagonists – no other fighter aircraft from either side could fly there, much less fight there. The two antagonists were, on the UN side, the new jet-powered, swept-wing North American Aviation (NAA) F-86 Sabre, and on the Communist side, their premier swept-wing jet fighter, the Mikoyan and Gurevich (MiG) 15.

The mission of the Soviet-built (and initially Russian-flown) MiG-15 was to guard the vital bridges spanning the wide Yalu River, the critical Supung hydro-electric powerplant up-river and the KPAF air bases between the Yalu and Pyongyang. The American F-86s were to protect the Boeing B-29 Superfortress bombers and a host of fighter-bombers attempting to destroy those targets. But even when such interdiction, strategic strike and airfield attack missions were not being flown, the Sabres regularly cruised into this aerial arena and frequently the MiG-15s launched to challenge them in battles totally isolated from the rest of the conflict.

Here, the best from both sides sparred and duelled, fought and killed – or died – in an arena almost completely detached from the World War I-like trench warfare far below to the south, and even from the results of the war as a whole. It was a battle much more for the prestige of the nations engaged – and the reputation of their respective aerospace industries – and for the glory of the fighter pilots involved than for its effect on the conduct or the outcome of the conflict.

Due to the duels' almost laboratory-like uniqueness and detachment, 60 years later we are able to effectively and conclusively examine and evaluate the two combatants – the F-86 Sabre and the MiG-15 – on both their individual and relative merits, and most importantly on their performance, and the performance of the men flying them, in mortal combat against one another.

Victory in an aerial battle is the culmination and consequence of a series of factors – the nature of the contest and the environment in which it is fought, the relative performance qualities of the competing aircraft and, most importantly, the training, experience and attitudes of the fighter pilots themselves. This book will examine all of those, and more. It will assess their relative merits, and their success or lack of it, based on the results of this combination of factors as it played out in the crucible of life-and-death combat, a crucible ensconced in the northwest corner of Korea known to the American Sabre pilots – and now to history – as "MiG Alley".

CHRONOLOGY

1945

May   Allied victory over Nazi Germany opens substantive high-speed, swept-wing aerodynamic research to American and Soviet aircraft designers.

November   USAAF approves NAA's proposal for the swept-wing XP-86.

1946

March   Soviet Union's V-VS issues requirement for a 1,000km/h jet fighter. Design of the MiG-15 begins.

1947

October 1   First flight of the NAA XP-86.

December 30   First flight of the MiG I-310/S-01 (MiG-15) prototype.

1948

May   First deliveries of production F-86A-1s to various US flight test organizations.

August 15   ROK formally established, claiming sovereignty over all of Korea.

September 9   DPRK formally established, also claiming sovereignty over all of Korea.

1949

February   First operational F-86As enter USAF service.

June   First operational MiG-15s enter V-VS service.

December   PRC established under Chairman Mao Zedong.

1950

June 25   DPRK army (KPA) invades South Korea.

August   KPA advances halted by US, ROK and UN forces at the Pusan Perimeter. Virtually destroyed, the KPAF is withdrawn to the PRC to rebuild.

September 15   US and ROK Marines land at Inchon, precipitating wholesale KPA collapse.

October 7   UN forces cross the 38th Parallel, intending to reunite the two Koreas under the ROK government.

October 8   Mao Zedong orders Chinese People's Volunteer Army (CPVA) into North Korea to stop UN advance towards Yalu.

October 11   Stalin agrees to send MiG-15s to provide air cover for the CPVA.

October 27   CPVA launches the first of four phased offensives designed to drive UN forces from the Korean Peninsula.

November 1   V-VS MiG-15s begin defensive patrols along the Yalu River.

November 9   HQ USAF despatches 4th Fighter Interceptor Wing (FIW) F-86s to Korea to counter the MiG-15.

The three XF-86 Sabre prototypes in flight together. (Duncan Curtis)

November 15	Soviet Far East Military District (FEMD) authorized to form the 64th IAK (*Istrebitelniy Aviatsionniy Korpus* – Fighter Aviation Corps) with two elite MiG-15 IADs (*Istrebitelnaya Aviatsionnaya Diviziyas* – Fighter Aviation Divisions).
December 15	4th Fighter Interceptor Group (FIG) establishes Detachment A with 32 F-86As at Kimpo AB.
December 17	First clash between Sabres and MiG-15s.

1951

January 2	4th FIG Det A evacuates Kimpo in the face of advancing CPVA forces.
January 4	CPVA forces capture Seoul.
February 20	UNC forces finally halt CPVA's "fourth phase offensive". UN counter-attacks push frontline back to approximate the 38th Parallel.
March 6	4th FIG resumes combat air patrols from Suwon AB.
April 2	324th IAD arrives at Andong's Langtao airfield to begin combat operations.
April 11	Gen Douglas MacArthur removed from commanding UNC by President Harry S. Truman.
May 28	303rd IAD arrives at nearby Dadonggou airfield to begin combat operations.
July 10	Ceasefire negotiations begin at Kaesong, and are eventually moved to Panmunjom.

August 26	First F-86E delivered to 4th FIW.
November 1	People's Liberation Army Air Force (PLAAF) establishes the 1st United Air Army (UAA) at Langtao, reinforcing 64th IAK with two PLAAF and one KPAF MiG-15 air divisions.
November 17	Final UNC ground offensive stabilizes front along what will become the Demilitarized Zone (DMZ).
November 22	USAF reinforces 4th FIG by converting the 51st FIG from F-80C to F-86E.

1952

January 25	324th IAD replaced by inexperienced 97th IAD at Langtao.
February 14	303rd IAD replaced by inexperienced 190th IAD at Dadonggou.
May 15	64th IAK reinforced with 133rd IAD at Andong.
June	First F-86F delivered to 51st FIW.
July	1st UAA assumes control of MiG-15 operations from 64th IAK.
July 30	190th IAD replaced by 216th IAD at Dadonggou.
August 27	97th IAD replaced by 32nd IAD at Langtao and Dapu.

1953

July 27	Ceasefire goes into effect, ending full-scale hostilities of the Korean War.

A Soviet V-VS MiG-15 unit lines up on the runway in preparation for a group takeoff. (NMUSAF)

DESIGN AND DEVELOPMENT

Had it not been for the advancing German aerodynamic research during the closing months of World War II, the air battles over the Yalu River would have been fought between straight-wing MiG-9s and their American contemporary, the Lockheed F-80C Shooting Star. Several notable German aeronautical engineers, such as the famous glider pioneer and tailless delta designer Alexander Lippisch, the flying wing visionaries Walter and Reimar Horten and the prolific and indomitable Wilhelm "Willi" Messerschmitt, led the world in developing swept-wing aircraft. In fact, Messerschmitt had fielded two revolutionary operational fighters, the Lippisch-designed, rocket-powered Me 163 Komet (Comet) and the twin-jet Me 262 Schwalbe (Swallow), both incorporating modest wing sweep to enable higher fighting speeds.

The most advanced, however, was the Focke-Wulf Ta 183 Huckebein (Hunchback). This aircraft beat Messerschmitt's P 1101 design in the February 1945 Emergency Fighter Competition – the Luftwaffe's search for a high performance, second-generation jet interceptor. The futuristic T-tailed Ta 183 was designed by Hans Multhopp and featured a short stubby fuselage with a round open-nose intake, a mid-mounted 40-degree swept wing and a sharply raked (60-degree sweep) vertical tail.

The project quickly progressed to the point where scale models were being used in the *Aerodynamische Versuchsanstalt* (AVA, the German equivalent of the US National Advisory Committee for Aeronautics [NACA], the forerunner of NASA) high-speed wind tunnel at Göttingen, collecting data for the refinement of the wing design. Multhopp's innovations were considered essential for "reducing drag dramatically as the aircraft approached the sonic barrier", and the AVA data supported his calculations that the jet could exceed 600mph (965km/h).

Later that spring, as the Third Reich finally collapsed, the invading American armies overran Bavaria, capturing Willy Messerschmitt, his Oberammergau secret projects complex, the 80 per cent complete P 1101 prototype, its aerodynamicist Woldemar Voigt and his design team. Hans Multhopp, the Bad Eilsen design offices of Focke-Wulf's head designer Kurt Tank, AVA's Göttingen facilities and Ta 183 models, design drawings and wind tunnel data fell into the hands of the advancing British forces, who shared these discoveries with the Americans. Closing in from the east, the Soviets confiscated a wealth of design plans – including Ta 183 materials – and wind tunnel data reports from the *Reichsluftfahrtministerium* (RLM) offices in Berlin, plus a vast storehouse of related materials at Rechlin and other captured Luftwaffe test facilities.

A wind tunnel model of Focke-Wulf's Ta 183 design proposal. (Tim Callaway Collection)

F-86A SABRE

By the time the captured swept-wing research information made it to the USA, NAA had already finalized its first offering for a jet-powered fighter. Responding to the US Army Air Forces (USAAF) request for a jet-powered escort fighter with dive-bombing capability, NAA designers, led by John "Lee" Atwood, de-navalized their NA-134 submission (which later became the US Navy's FJ-1 Fury) to answer the call. The resulting NA-140 used the laminar flow wing of the war-winning P-51D Mustang in a conventional layout around a General Electric (GE, later Allison) J35 axial-flow jet engine.

Recognizing that the design could not meet the USAAF requirement for a 600mph top speed, and realizing that the newly acquired German research data promised superior high speed performance, NAA President James H. "Dutch" Kindelberger decided to pass on this opportunity – which was won by Lockheed's P-80. Instead, he ordered that the NA-140 be redesigned using the nascent information to develop a higher speed wing.

Despite having signed a contract for three straight-wing XP-86s in May 1944, the NAA's revised proposal for a new all-swept NA-140 design was submitted in September 1945 and accepted by the USAAF two months later. The benefits of sweeping the wing were to reduce the effects of air's compressibility (whose mounting density as airspeed increased precluded straight wings from achieving supersonic flight

An NAA model of the NA-140 design proposal, circa 1945. This was an adaptation of the company's NA-134 proposal, which was submitted to the US Navy and developed into the FJ-1 Fury. (NAA via Duncan Curtis)

in all but the most extreme situations), delay the formation of sonic shock waves, lower the drag coefficient and, lastly, increase the critical Mach number. This last element is the aircraft's speed (relative to the speed of sound) at which the "relative wind speed" reaches Mach 1 and the sonic compression ("shock") wave attaches to the wing's surface. Several undesirable consequences are affected, the most significant of which is "control reversal" where the airflow atop the wing, by changing velocity after passing through the compression wave, imparts reverse reactions to any control surface deflections. So the higher the design's critical Mach number, the better, because the consequences for exceeding it were generally catastrophic.

However desirous wing sweep was for high-speed flight, it was just as deleterious on low-speed performance. Swept wings stalled at significantly higher speeds, violently and inconsistently, and aileron effectiveness deteriorated markedly as airspeed decreased. Consequently, Atwood's team eschewed Multhopp's rather extreme approach and used a moderate 35-degree sweepback, employing 75 per cent span leading edge "slats" to increase lift at lower speeds. Developed initially by Handley Page, but used to great advantage by Messerschmitt's superb Bf 109 fighter and other high-performance aircraft, slats are cambered leading edges that extend forward at lower speeds/higher angle-of-attack (by the forward shift of the wing's lifting forces), thereby increasing the wing's chord. This increases the wing's surface area and the amount of lift it produces, thus lowering the stalling speed of the aircraft.

NAA was able to achieve a thin wing – 11 per cent thickness-to-chord (sometimes called "fineness") ratio at the root, tapering to ten per cent at the tip – through superior American manufacturing techniques, using machine-milled, double-layer skins to avoid the bulkier traditional ribs and stringer construction. The leading edge slats, originally built in four sections, were soon extended to 90 per cent span, the panels bolted together as one long piece. The wing also incorporated large-area integral fuel tanks and had large ailerons, hydraulically boosted to overcome the great aerodynamic forces experienced at near-Mach speeds.

The fuselage, the design of which was already well developed, included an ejection seat, a roomy, pressurized cockpit and a spectacular all-round view through a streamlined teardrop-shaped "bubble" canopy. The tail surfaces were also swept 35 degrees and

F-86F-1 SABRE

37ft 6in

14ft 8in

37ft 1in

mounted hydraulically-boosted elevators that greatly aided control at and beyond the critical Mach number of 0.95 – indicated by a "red line" on the Mach indicator.

When the first XP-86 took to the air on October 1, 1947, its high-speed flight characteristics were flawless. Test pilot George S. Welch said "the plane's so clean you never have any trouble. [It's] reduced drag to a minimum and you don't have to worry about the effects of compressibility shock waves". With the 3,950lb thrust Allison J35-A-5 installed, the jet attained a level speed of 618mph (995km/h) at 14,000ft (4,267m), and achieved Mach 1 in a shallow dive on March 1, 1948. Because the aircraft approached static instability at that point in its flight envelope, control was marginal and required diligent concentration and sensitive, precise pilot inputs. Nevertheless, Welch was pleased there were no pronounced ill effects on handling above critical Mach.

The design, proposed for production as the NA-151, was so promising that the USAAF signed a contract for 33 P-86As in November 1946, increasing the quantity to 221 in December. The first production version was powered by the 4,850lb thrust J47-GE-1 and featured two underwing hardpoints for carrying 1,000lb (453.6kg) bombs, 120 US gallon (454 liter) drop tanks or 16 5-in (127mm) rockets. Its armament was the tried-and-true combination of six Colt-Browning AN/M-3 0.50-in (12.7mm) machine guns, paired with the gyro-stabilized, lead-computing Mk 18 optical gunsight that had proven to be so effective on late-model P-51s in World War II.

The first production Sabre flew in May 1948, and the following month the newly-formed US Air Force (USAF) changed the fighter's designation to F-86A. The first batch – the original 33 jets produced as F-86A-1s – were primarily used in various testing and research programs by NAA, the NACA and the USAF. Operational service began the next year when the famous 94th "Hat in the Ring" Fighter Squadron (FS) received ten F-86A-1s in February-March. The other squadrons of the 1st FG soon followed suit, 72 (of the 188) F-86A-5s replacing their straight-wing F-80s by early August.

While the 1st FG protected the concentration of America's burgeoning aerospace industries in the Los Angeles area, the next 75 jets went to the 4th FG (the 4th FG/FW

F-86A-5s of the 1st FIG's 27th FIS in their hangar at George AFB, California, in August 1950. (Duncan Curtis)

was re-titled the 4th FIG/FIW in January 1949), headquartered at Langley Air Force Base (AFB), Virginia, and responsible for defending Washington, DC. The first examples arrived in June 1949, and the unit was fully converted by the autumn.

Meanwhile, that February, the USAF ordered another 333 F-86A-5s. These were used to equip three more fighter groups, as well as "The Fighter School" (later to become the 57th FW) at Nellis AFB, Las Vegas, Nevada. The most historically significant of the operational units was the Selfridge AFB, Michigan, based 56th FIG, which was responsible for defending the expansive American automotive industry in the Detroit area. By the time DPRK Prime Minister Kim Il-Sung surprised the West with his invasion of South Korea, the USAF had five frontline fighter wings, each with 75 new F-86As, in its order of battle.

The lack of significant modification after the production of the first 530 copies is strong testament to the soundness of Atwood's original design. In fact, the main difficulty was not with the airframe, but with GE's J47 turbojet. Spinning at 7,700rpm (military power setting), the turbine wheel would occasionally fly apart, frequently resulting in the loss of the aircraft. Improvement was noted with the installation of the 5,200lb thrust J47-GE-13 engine, a field modification completed fleet-wide on frontline jets by May 1950.

Also in development since November 1949 was a major improvement to enhance controllability at and beyond critical Mach number. Called the "all-flying tail" or "stabilator" (combination horizontal stabilizer and elevator), it was introduced on the NA-170/F-86E. Fully hydraulically powered and complete with an "artificial feel" system for tactile control force feedback to the pilot, the "all-flying tail" was relatively simple and very effective, permitting full control beyond "red line". Impressed, the USAF ordered 111 F-86Es in January 1950.

The final airframe change – introduced with the F-86F-25/30 – was the famous "6-3 wing". While the slats were critical for low-speed control, the original "5 AR" (aspect ratio [span to chord] of 4.79:1) wing was a compromise for Atwood's design team. From the beginning a "6 AR wing" was desired because the higher aspect ratio provided a much more advantageous lift/drag ratio. But even with leading edge slats, the "6 AR wing" was prone to violent pitch up tendencies, so the less efficient "5 AR" planform was used. However, with the "all-flying" stabilator overcoming this vice, NAA was able to retro-create the more desirous "6 AR wing" by replacing the slats with a "hard" leading edge that extended the wing's chord six inches (152mm) at the root and three inches (76mm) at the tip (hence the "6-3" moniker). This, plus the 12-inch (305mm) tip extensions introduced on the F-86F-40, gave the design essentially a "6 AR wing."

In the high altitude combats in "MiG Alley", the new wing provided marginally higher top end speeds and, more importantly, it significantly enhanced the Sabre's maneuverability, enabling tighter turns in the thin air at high Mach. But this would come later, after the first encounters with the surprisingly agile and powerful MiG-15 highlighted the need for better performance and maneuverability from what was already America's pre-eminent jet fighter.

MiG-15

While the NAA designers had the challenge of applying swept-wing technology to an existing design proposal, the aeronautical engineers at the MiG experimental design bureau (*Opytno-Konstrooktorskoye Byuro*, or OKB) had to start from scratch. They began with the March 1946 *Voenno-Vozdushnye Sily* (literally, "Military Air Forces" or V-VS, the Soviet Union's tactical air force) requirement for a 621mph (1,000km/h) fighter able to fly up to an altitude of 45,932ft (14,000m), operate from unimproved airfields and perform ground attack as well as intercept missions. The speed requirement necessitated jet propulsion and swept wings.

While the MiG OKB had conducted some studies on swept wings and high-speed flight, the captured German research materials – and especially the German aeronautical engineers deported to the USSR to help develop the Soviet Union's most advanced post-war aircraft – were an enormous boon. Russian aviation historians marginalize the influence of the Ta 183 and other late Nazi designs, but the resulting product speaks for itself; a short, round fuselage with a straight-through installation of the Soviet-copied Junkers Jumo 004A Orkan (Hurricane) jet engine, sharply swept mid-mounted wing and T-tail. However, the MiG designers, in order to reduce the frontal area and resulting profile (or form) drag, eliminated the high-drag "hunchback" – the cockpit and fuel tanks mounted atop the air intake tunnel and engine in the

Ta 183 design – by "pushing it down" between the bifurcated air ducts ahead of the engine, making the aircraft commensurately longer than the German concept.

From the very beginning the design was a sequence of compromises. The axial-flow Jumo copy, designated the RD-10, proved a poor choice, producing only 1,984lb (900kg) of thrust. So a three-man delegation, including Mikoyan and engine designer Vladimir Y. Klimov, went to the UK and acquired 25 centrifugal-flow Rolls-Royce Nenes through the British Labour government's socialist Board of Trade President and ambassador to the USSR in 1940-42, Stafford Cripps. Reportedly, the British government agreed to this sale on the condition that the engines would "not be used for military purposes". Ironically, the largest military use of any version of the Nene was the Klimov RD-45. Additionally, Rolls-Royce later attempted to claim £207 million in license fees from the Soviet government, but without success. Klimov quickly had his Plant No. 45 reverse-engineer the engine and began producing the 5,005lb (2,270kg) thrust Nene 2 as the RD-45F shortly thereafter.

Significantly, the RD-45F's centrifugal compressor had a diameter more than 18 inches (0.5m) greater than the axial-flow RD-10, thus requiring the "fattening" of the MiG's fuselage to accept the new engine. In flight a short, rotund body is less stable directionally (yaw), resulting in the need for an enlarged vertical fin to keep it flying straight. The engine's jet pipe was kept short to reduce rear fuselage component temperatures, resulting in an exaggerated 56-degree rake to the vertical stabilizer to place the rudder as far aft as possible.

However, a large tail also imparts longitudinal (roll) stability, reducing a fighter's ability to bank quickly. The reduced roll authority was offset by applying two degrees anhedral to the wings (dihedral enhances roll stability, anhedral reduces it). Unwilling to accept the severe low-speed handling penalties of Multhopp's bold sweepback, the MiG OKB settled on a more moderate 37-degree sweep. It is commonly believed that the MiG-15 had a 35-degree wing sweep, but this was an engineer's measurement at one-quarter chord, not leading edge sweep.

Using three-spar, stressed skin over ribs and stringer construction, the wing had an 11 per cent thickness ratio from the landing gear hinge point outboard, with slightly increasing wingform thickness inboard to accommodate the large, low-pressure tires needed for operations from unsurfaced airstrips – the wing's aspect ratio was very similar to the F-86A's wing, at 4.85:1.

This combination resulted in significant "spanwise flow", where the air is deflected outwards towards the wingtip, thus reducing lift, decreasing aileron effectiveness and causing premature stall at the wingtip. Consequently, two tall, full chord "wing fences" were needed to keep the airflow going parallel to the longitudinal axis of the aircraft.

The horizontal stabilizer was swept 40 degrees, and being structurally difficult to fit atop the fin, it was set two-thirds up the vertical stabilizer and mounted as far aft as possible. This was to provide the greatest possible pitching moment (for pulling G and turning tightly) so that the fighter was as maneuverable as possible for air-to-air combat.

The prototype – designated I-310 (serial S-01) – was first flown on December 30, 1947 by V. N. Yuganov, and not surprisingly it was found to be "generally satisfactory, but pulling too much G caused a sudden flick into a spin [due to limited yaw stability/ control] and there were problems with yaw and roll". Additionally, the deep-set cockpit – done to minimize the height, size and resultant form drag from the low-profile bubble canopy – resulted in very poor forward visibility at slow speeds, such as on final approach for landing.

Nevertheless, the exigencies of the developing Cold War pushed the project forward. Manufacturer's tests were completed three months later and the (now) two prototypes were transferred to the V-VS Scientific Research Institute (Russian abbreviation NII) near Moscow for State acceptance trials. In December 1948, even before these were completed, the V-VS commander ordered the type into full-scale production.

Produced during the first half of the next year, the initial batch was used to train V-VS instructor pilots. Because of its revolutionary high performance and the lack of two-seat trainers at this early stage – Yak-17UTI production was just starting about this time, but MiG-15UTI production would not begin until about 18 months later

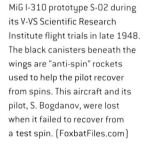

MiG I-310 prototype S-02 during its V-VS Scientific Research Institute flight trials in late 1948. The black canisters beneath the wings are "anti-spin" rockets used to help the pilot recover from spins. This aircraft and its pilot, S. Bogdanov, were lost when it failed to recover from a test spin. (FoxbatFiles.com)

The first MiG-15 of the small initial production batch – designated the MiG-15(S) by the MiG OKB – during acceptance trials. Note the small speedbrake (extended) added to the tailpipe almost as an after-thought. (FoxbatFiles.com)

– NII test pilots were employed to teach the first instructor pilots, many of the latter having some experience flying the far more primitive straight-wing MiG-9.

The first unit to receive the initial batch, designated the MiG-15(S) by the OKB, was the elite 324th IAD at Kubinka air base (AB), near Moscow. Its pilots were handpicked, 75 per cent of them being veterans of the Great Patriotic War (World War II), and they were considered the best trained and most experienced in the V-VS. Its 29th GvIAP (*Gvardeyskiy Istrebitelniy Aviatsionniy Polk* – Guards Fighter Aviation Regiment) was the first unit to receive the new MiG-15, conducting the operational evaluation of the jet, while its 196th IAP (*Istrebitelniy Aviatsionniy Polk* – Fighter Aviation Regiment) tested the competing Lavochkin La-15 design. The latter was soon released for service and began equipping the 192nd IAD, allowing the 196th IAP to convert to the MiG-15. The 324th IAD's third regiment, the 176th IAP, flew the straight-wing Yak-15 until early 1950, when it too converted to the vastly superior swept-wing MiG.

The Soviets showed off their newly developed technology by including the 324th IAD's MiG-15s in their 1949 May Day military display, flying a huge formation of

Being the premier MiG-15 unit, the elite 324th IAD formed a display team to show off its new jet fighters, thrilling crowds at "open days" and impressing dignitaries with "air parades". These displays led to the 324th being derided as the *paradnaya divisiya* ("parade division") by other IADs in the V-VS. Pilots from the division would soon get the opportunity to show off their tactical prowess as well. (Tim Callaway Collection)

MiG-15bis

35ft 2in

12ft 1.67in

33ft 1in

45 jets over Red Square. At the July Tushino airshow 52 of the type paraded overhead, and during the November 7 "October Revolution Celebration" 90 MiG-15s participated in the fly-by. Additionally, the 324th IAD formed a colorful and exciting aerial demonstration team that frequently performed at other air displays.

By the summer of 1950 the 324th was finally operational on the early version of the new jet fighter, which had been in full-scale production for a year. It featured hydraulically-boosted ailerons, a number of internal refinements and its armament was standardized with a single slow-firing (400 rounds per minute) but heavy-hitting 37mm Nudel'man N-37D cannon and two 23mm Nudel'man-Suranov NS-23KM (550 rounds per minute) weapons, paired with the World War II-standard ASP-1N gyroscopic gunsight.

The type was also issued to the 151st GvIAD (*Gvardeyskiy Istrebitelniy Aviatsionniy Diviziya* – Guards Fighter Aviation Division), an La-11 unit stationed nearby at Kalinin AB, and the 303rd "Smolensk Order of Red Banner" IAD, which moved to Yaroslavl' (also near Moscow) for the conversion. Both of these units became combat-ready in mid-1950. By the time Prime Minister Kim Il-Sung initiated his invasion of South Korea, the V-VS had three fighter divisions, each with 120 new MiG-15s, on its order of battle, with others following closely behind.

Meanwhile, Klimov's development of the Nene had continued. By making significant changes to the compressor section, as well as other improvements, his factory had been able to develop a much more powerful (5,922lb/2,700kg thrust) derivative in 1949. Since this engine was a significant departure from its predecessor, the powerplant warranted its own designation. It duly became the Klimov VK-1A. The compressor section redesign resulted in an even larger diameter, but by modifying the airframe's internal structure, this was accommodated without making the aircraft's body even "fatter". The mounting of the VK-1A, plus other airframe improvements such as 21 per cent larger ailerons to enhance roll authority, redesigned speedbrakes to eliminate a pitch-up moment experienced upon deployment and other aerodynamic enhancements, led to the creation of the definitive version of the type, called the MiG-15(SD) by the OKB.

Manufacturer's tests were completed in September 1949, and the much-improved variant went to NII for V-VS acceptance tests, which were completed by the end of the year. Immediately ordered into full-scale production, the variant was designated the MiG-15bis by the V-VS. Examples began to reach frontline units in mid-1950.

OPPOSITE
MiG-15bis 0715321 was completed at Novosibirsk's Factory No. 153 in September 1950 and was immediately sent to the 50th IAD at Xiansilipu airfield, near Dalian, in China. In January 1951 the fighter was transferred to the 151st GvIAD, which was busy training PLAAF pilots. At this point the V-VS command realized that having its two elite air divisions being bested over the Yalu by F-86s while flying the type's earlier variant, when Chinese pilots were being trained on the later, better version did not make good sense, so the units swapped their entire inventories. "721" was duly sent to the 324th IAD's 176th GvIAP for combat duties, and it was subsequently used to good effect by Capt Sergei "Baida" Kramarenko. Indeed, he claimed eight of his 13 accredited victories – two RAAF Meteor F 8s, two USAF F-84s and four F-86s – in the aircraft, after which it was handed down through several IAPs that later replaced the original elite units.

TECHNICAL
SPECIFICATIONS

F-86A SABRE

Spurred on by the intensity and urgency of World War II – a global war in which unconditional surrender or total destruction were the only acceptable outcomes – aviation technology advanced by leaps and bounds through the 1940s. Pre-eminent among the attributes of developing designs, at least as far as the media and public were concerned, was "top speed" and maximum (max) altitude.

When the XP-86 took to the skies over southern California in late 1947 it certainly did not disappoint. In fact, the next year the USAF sought to break the world air speed record – then held by the US Navy's rocket-powered Douglas D-558-1 Skyrocket research aircraft – using its new operational jet fighter. On September 14, at Muroc Dry Lake, Maj Robert L. Johnson took F-86A-1 47-611 six times through a 3km (1.86 miles) Federation Aeronautique Internationale (FAI) course at a height of approximately 100ft (30.5m) to set the new record at 670.981mph (1,079km/h).

Additionally, test pilots "toyed" with the "sonic barrier" several times during the jet's early days. In November 1947, NACA personnel clocked Welch at Mach 1.03 at 35,000ft (10,668m) only five weeks after Chuck Yeager and the Bell XS-1 officially achieved this feat. While according to the USAF the XP-86's maximum speed was Mach 0.937, for its own publicity, on 26 April the next year, NAA demonstrated that

the nation's newest jet fighter could indeed break the "sound barrier" when it did so in a dramatic, thunderclap fashion over Los Angeles, California.

These events confirmed that, aerodynamically, the Sabre was a very "slick" (low drag) design enabling excellent acceleration downhill, even with a Flight Manual imposed "Limit Mach" (later known as Velocity Never Exceed [V_{NE}]) of 0.95M. It remained stable beyond "red-line", although flight control was "touchy" in that regime. While control reversal was felt by pilots when above V_{NE}, the F-86A's hydraulically-boosted elevators – and later the F-86E's "irreversible, all-flying" stabilator – minimized its effects to such an extent that it was fully controllable even on the other side of "red line."

While the aviation press, NAA's marketing hype and the USAF's public pronouncements all touted the new jet's top speed and max altitude, operationally, these two attributes only got the pilot to his target quickly and, hopefully, with a

F-86A armament – six Browning AN/M-3 0.50-cal. machine guns. The weapons' ammunition canisters fitted into the belly bay beneath the guns, each "ammo can" holding 300 rounds maximum. The spent shell casings were collected in a canvas bag in the nose wheel well, and this was removed and emptied after flight. (Jerry Scutts via Warren Thompson)

The advanced J-1 fire control system – comprising the A-1C(M) gunsight and the AN/APG-30 radar – mounted immediately in front of the cockpit was a delicate piece of high-tech equipment prone to frequent failures, and it was difficult to maintain in Korea's primitive operating conditions. (Bill Nowadnick via Warren Thompson)

favorable height advantage. Once there, he relied on the fighter's maneuverability to get into a position to shoot at the target, and its weapons suite to do so. Because of its quick control responses, the F-86A was initially considered a very maneuverable fighter, especially for a fast, swept-wing jet, although it quite naturally had much wider "turning circles" than straight-wing and propeller-driven aircraft due to its much greater airspeeds.

Following the Korean War the USAF Fighter Weapons School at Nellis AFB began to develop – beginning with Maj John Boyd's pioneering demonstrations using the F-86 – two concepts that later proved useful in assessing a fighter's maneuverability potential. These were wing loading and thrust-to-weight ratio. Even though not in vogue in 1950, they are terms that are useful when comparing the Sabre with the MiG-15 (in the following section).

F-86 SABRE MACHINE GUNS

Except for eight F-86F-2s, all versions of the Sabre used in Korea were equipped with six Colt-Browning AN/M-3 0.50-cal. (12.7mm) machine guns, three mounted on either side of the nose. Equipped with an electrically boosted ammunition feed system, the improved version of World War II's AN/M-2 had a cyclic rate-of-fire of 1,200 rounds per minute. While the maximum effective range was 2,000ft, the guns were harmonized (their bullet streams converged) at 1,200ft ahead of the aircraft, making the 850-1,200ft range the Sabre's most lethal envelope. The ammunition canisters stored beneath the guns could accommodate 300 rounds for each weapon, but usually the best pilots had them filled with 267 rounds because, if completely filled, the topmost "row of bullets" could jam against the top of the can on the very first squeeze of the trigger.

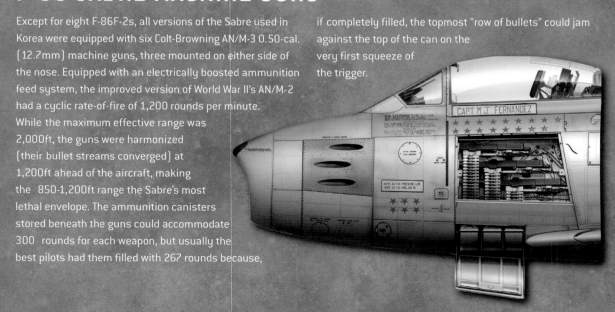

The F-86A's combat weight (pilot, parachute, full armament, 60 per cent fuel and no external stores) was approximately 12,123lbs (6,498kg), giving it a wing loading of 44.25lbs/sq ft and a thrust-to-weight ratio of 0.45:1. The "E-model" airframe included additional equipment and a number of enhancements that added 462lbs (210kg) using the same engine, so its wing loading was increased to 45.93lbs/sq ft and thrust-to-weight ratio dwindled to 0.43:1. Naturally, the newer model had slightly less performance – about two per cent in most categories.

The F-86A's wing was a compromise providing excellent straight-line speed at all altitudes, but generating relatively poor turning performance at high Mach and high altitude. At lower altitudes, in thicker air – below 30,000ft (9,144m) and 0.80 Mach (about 330mph indicated airspeed [IAS]) – the Sabre's turning performance improved because, at that speed, if the Sabre pilot was pulling G, the leading edge slats would automatically extend, creating a larger wing, more lift and a tighter radius/faster rate turn.

The Sabre "jock's" "front office" – the cockpit of an F-86A-5. The olive-colored apparatus mounted atop the glare shield is the A-1C(M) gunsight, projecting its reticule on the angled "combining glass" above it. (Duncan Curtis)

Since the F-86 was superior to all known adversaries (the MiG-15 was not one of these pre-December 1950), it was expected to use its high-altitude/high-Mach performance to close with the enemy with a height advantage. The Sabre would then descend upon its foes and begin maneuvering, its slats enabling the jet to turn with the enemy fighters and arrive at "guns solution" to begin firing at them.

For this third part of the equation, the F-86A-5 was equipped with six Colt-Browning AN/M-3 0.50-cal. machine guns, and initially had the US Navy's World War II-vintage Mk 18 (an improved version of the USAAF's K-14) gyro-stabilized gunsight. Gyro-stabilization compensated for the Gs that the pilot was pulling at that moment, thus providing sufficient "lead" (pulling the nose to point well ahead of the target) to allow for the "trajectory shift" that the bullet stream experienced upon exiting the muzzles of the guns under G.

Eventually, emerging radar technology made the Sabre's weapons extremely accurate. The first 309 of the second batch of F-86A-5s were built to mount the new Sperry A-1B lead-computing gunsight linked with the S-band AN/APG-5C range-only radar. The latter, originally designed for directing the guns of B-17s and B-24s, was effective out to 5,400ft (1,646m) and automatically provided distance data to the gunsight, which in turn computed the lead required to compensate for "gravity drop" of the bullets at that distance.

There were significant problems with adapting a relatively sedately-flying bomber's gunlaying radar to the more dynamic fighter environment, and the A-1B experienced chronic "pipper jitter" when the Brownings were fired. This led to the last 24 jets in this batch featuring the improved A-1C(M) (M for "modified") gunsight linked to GE's new X-band AN/APG-30 radar, which was effective out to 9,000ft (2,743m). Retrofitted in the field to earlier aircraft, these jets duly became F-86A-7s.

However, this technically sophisticated package had two major disadvantages. Firstly, below an altitude of 6,000ft (1,829m) the radar registered the distance to the ground rather than to the target, making it worthless in low-level engagements. Secondly, and more importantly, the radar's early vacuum-tube technology could easily be damaged by sharp jolts, and being mounted in the tip of the nose intake ring, it suffered from the shocks of landing and the incessant vibrations caused by taxiing over the rough pierced steel planking (PSP) when going to and from the parking revetments. Furthermore, due to Korea's primitive field conditions, a lack of test equipment and few spare parts, the radar was difficult to maintain, so many "Sabre jocks" had the 200lbs (90.7kg) of "luxury gadgets" removed to improve their jet's performance.

The biggest weakness of the F-86 was that the Brownings' weight of fire and impact energy were relatively light. While sufficient at lower speeds and lower altitude, at high Mach the F-86 "jock" had to get very close to his target to be effective – something that was exceedingly difficult to do during dynamic, high-speed combat at high altitudes.

The "front office" of the Sabre was a spacious fit, with instruments arrayed logically and controls readily at hand. Even before ergonomics were in vogue, NAA arranged an almost intuitive layout that made the aircraft easy to fly. The pilot sat high in the cockpit, beneath a clear, capacious canopy granting him exceptional all-round and downward vision, easily enabling him to twist about to "check six" (the six o'clock position behind the aircraft, the attacker's typical approach angle). Like the Mustang a generation before it, the Sabre was truly a fighter pilot's airplane.

As one British aviation historian remarked years after the Sabre entered service with the Royal Air Force, "NAA had created a fighter that handled superbly and needed virtually no modification. At the same time the company's engineering excellence made it a model of hardware design, so that eight years later British fighter pilots and designers still marvelled at the profusion of slick switches and buttons which all worked! Even the blown-plastics canopy was beyond the technology of other countries".

MiG-15

The Sabre's adversary, on the other hand, impressed with sheer performance. "The MiG-15 exceeded all our expectations" one Russian fighter pilot confirmed. "My first flight in a MiG-15 left an indelible impression on me. After a push forward on the throttle, the airplane literally darted away, and in a few seconds soared up. The altimeter was quickly counting the tens of meters. It was a bit hard to manipulate the ailerons – the airplane tended to bank reluctantly in response to sideward movements of the [control] stick, but willingly responded to the back and forth stick movements and would easily switch from ascent or descent".

For a hastily conceived, mass produced modern jet fighter, in spite of its multitude of compromises, the MiG-15 proved to be a remarkably fast, agile and heavily armed interceptor. Overall, its structure was relatively light, and mating it to a powerful jet engine resulted in a superior thrust-to-weight ratio (0.60:1 for the MiG-15bis) that was some 30 per cent better than the Sabre. This gave it a dramatic rate of climb – 4.62 minutes to get to 32,800ft (10,000m) – and a service ceiling fully 2,500-3,500ft (750-1,055m) above the F-86. As a result, the initial height advantage went to the MiG.

While the top speed of the two jets seemed equally matched, at high altitudes it is Mach that counts, and the MiG-15 suffered from a relatively low critical Mach number (V_{NE}) of 0.92. Above this speed directional stability deteriorated markedly, resulting in yawing ("snaking") from side to side – something the jet's unboosted rudder could not correct. Even the hydraulically boosted ailerons were hard to actuate at high speeds, taking both hands to move (as if the stick was "stuck in cement"), and resulting in an excruciatingly slow roll rate. Most critically, because of the MiG-15's light construction and poor quality control at the various assembly plants building the aircraft, the wings rarely matched! And near critical Mach, they tended to "warp" due to insufficient stiffness and inconsistent sonic wave attachments, resulting in sudden uncommanded rolling moments (called valezhka, or "wing drop") that could only be controlled by slowing down.

Additionally, above 0.92M, the unboosted elevators experienced control reversal due to sonic wave attachment to the tailplane surface, dramatically changing its control dynamics. Frequently, this would cause sharp pitch-up moments if any "back stick" was applied to pull out of high-speed dives or to initiate a defensive turn. Many times – in at least 56 cases documented during combat – the MiG was seen to "depart controlled flight", the aircraft pitching up violently into a high speed stall and the yawing moment causing it to "swap ends" and snap into a spin. These were frequently unrecoverable, resulting in the loss of 40 aircraft. In numerous other instances the sharp pitch-up would cause an "over-G" in which G-forces in excess of those for which the airframe was stressed would bend and distort the empennage – some were even seen to shed wings or tail assemblies.

This issue became so critical that the MiG-15bis was soon retrofitted with a new Mach indicator – the M-0.92 – that had an automatic trigger deploying the speedbrakes

MiG-15bis weapons suite – one N-37 (far side) and two NR-23s (near side), mounted on a single retractable tray complete with ammunition canisters. This allowed for quick "combat turnarounds", which meant that in less than a minute the whole tray could be winched down, disconnected from the cables and replaced by a pre-loaded tray that came complete with new weapons. (Tim Callaway Collection)

at 0.92M to slow the jet to below "red line" so that it would not "self-destruct". In the interim, the early MiG-15s were limited by a flight manual restriction to 1,100km/h (683.5mph).

In high altitude maneuvering at slower speeds the MiG had a noticeable turning advantage over the Sabre. The lighter wing loadings of the early MiG-15 gave it a tighter, faster turn and the more powerful VK-1A engine of the MiG-15bis ensured that the later model could sustain its turn longer, losing less altitude, and was able to zoom and power its way back up, out of reach, to heights beyond the Sabre's ceiling.

However, once below 30,000ft (9,144m), if the MiG pilot turned so aggressively that he shed airspeed, the Sabre's leading edge slats provided a great advantage. In a turning fight below 330mph IAS (530km/h) the MiG pilot was doomed. Additionally, the need for an anti-G suit (wrapped like Old Western cowboy "chaps" around the calves, thighs and gut to squeeze the blood back up to the heart and brain under G) was another

MiG-15bis CANNON

After July 1951, the MiG-15bis featured an upgraded weapons suite that saw a pair of Nudel'man-Rikhter NR-23s replacing the earlier MiG-15's World War II-vintage NS-23s. The improved 23mm cannon had mechanical improvements designed to increase the rate-of-fire to 850 rounds per minute, but in practice normally only 650 rounds per minute was achievable. While both the N-37D and NR-23 had relatively low muzzle velocity (both approximately 2,300ft-per-second), the impact force of the explosive cannon shells could be devastating. The NR-23s were limited to a 5.3-second burst of fire, and usually only one- to two-second "sighting bursts" were used until hits were achieved, then longer bursts were fired. The NR-23s each carried 80 rounds, and once an effective firing solution was obtained the N-37D's 40 rounds would be used to destroy the target.

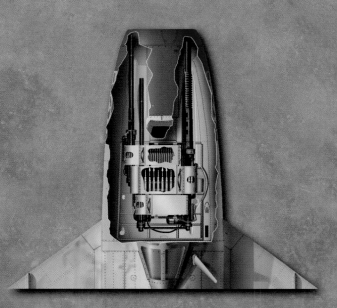

afterthought. The PPK-1 system (-1.75 to +8 G) was added only to the later batches of the MiG-15bis after the Korean War had ended, this deficiency giving the Sabre pilot a significant physical advantage – his body could sustain and endure the heavy Gs – as well as an aerodynamic one.

Finally, the MiG was hamstrung by its weapons suite. During its early development, when the La-15 initially appeared to be a viable stablemate to the MiG-15 in the V-VS arsenal, both jets were ordered into production. The Lavochkin's superior maneuverability made it the command's choice for its tactical fighter, while the MiG's heavier armament favored its use as a strategic interceptor and "bomber destroyer". In fact the latter's 37mm cannon was tested against an American B-29 bomber (interned during World War II) and its Tupolev Tu-4 "Bull" clone. Soviet engineers judged that the hefty 26.5 ounce (1.66lb/0.75kg) high explosive (HE) shell could bring down the B-29 with two hits. Tests with the NS-23 determined that it took eight hits to shoot down a B-29, but just two to bring down a typical American fighter type (F-80, F-84 or F-86) aircraft.

Eventually the La-15 had to be discarded primarily because of its complexity and commensurate expense of manufacture. Needing to provide large numbers of modern jet fighters to the Chinese, as well as upgrade its own forces as rapidly as possible, the Soviets could only afford to produce one type. Since the MiG-15 could bring down an atomic bomb-carrying B-29 with its N-37 – the La-15 only had NS-23s – it was picked to fill both the bomber interceptor and tactical fighter roles.

The MiG-15's 23mm and 37mm HE cannon shells could do substantial damage when they hit, but the F-86's robust construction could absorb a lot of punishment. Here, Maj Curtis L. Utterback's F-86A is shown after it was hit in the left flap. (Dean Juhlin via Warren Thompson)

The MiG-15 cockpit was a cluttered, cramped and confining place to work. The brown ball-shaped object at the top of the photo is the cushion provided to keep the pilot's head from being injured by the ASP gunsight in the event of a sudden (crash-like) deceleration. (NMUSAF)

The single, slow-firing N-37 and twin 23mm cannon had excellent effective range – about 3,050ft (1,000m) – but had dissimilar ballistic trajectories. Some Sabre pilots had the unnerving experience of seeing 23mm shells passing overhead while 37mm rounds flew by underneath! Worse, at speeds above 800km/h (499mph) the aim-point ("pipper") of the World War II-vintage ASP-1N gunsight, which was a reverse-engineered RAF Mk 2D gunsight designed for use with British 0.303-in. machine guns in Hurricanes and Spitfires, was no longer indicating where the cannon shells were going! Additionally it had to be set by hand (by twisting the throttle, known as "stadiametric ranging") based on the pilot's visual range estimation.

These weapons deficiencies resulted in the MiG pilot having to get close and fire one or two "sighting bursts", then use tracers to correct his aim to the target. In fact, many a "Sabre jock" was awarded membership of the "Six O'clock Club" for having been shot at from behind and, upon seeing the "flaming golf balls" flying past his aircraft, executing a sharp "break turn" that defeated the attack, enabling him to survive. When the MiG pilot attempted to follow, the combination of rolling into bank and adding G caused the ASP's gyro to "tumble" at 3-4 Gs, making it completely unusable in subsequent attacks. The later ASP-3N, which was designed to project the trajectory of the NS-23 cannon rounds and could be stowed to reduce head injuries in forced or heavy landings, had identical propensities.

Furthermore, the exaggerated Korean War MiG-15 "kill claims" made by the Soviets were largely because the S-13 gun camera was not aligned with either the gunsight or either cannons' ballistics. It ran only while the firing buttons were depressed, these frequently being released – ending the filming – about the time the shells were arriving at the target's range, so the actual effects of the shooting were not recorded. Film "graders" commonly included unit commanders and political commissars who would confirm a "kill" – sometimes even if one had not been claimed by the pilot – when the camera's crosshairs touched the target for two movie frames. That meant, as one Russian historian admits, "that the results of combat by [MiG-15] divisions were subject to greater errors", and consequently units generously exaggerated their official "kill" claims.

Finally, the pilot's position in the cockpit was cramped and confining, sitting low with little visibility downward and none to the rear. The "bubble" canopy had heavy framing mating its two pieces behind the pilot's head, and this – coupled with restrictions to turning around in the cockpit – resulted in an inability to "check six". Ergonomics were a nightmare for the pilot. In fact, the early version used a bank of push-button type circuit breakers where all the "switches" were grouped together on the right forward panel, forcing the pilot to take his hand off the control column to actuate them. Known as the "Russian accordion", it was easy to push the wrong one – especially under G. Rightly so, these were later replaced with conventional toggle switches.

All things considered, if given sufficient warning via the air defense radar and observers' net, the MiG-15 could reach a superior height (called a "perch") before the F-86s arrived in the area, and were thus able to dictate whether, where, when and from what approach angle an engagement would be initiated. Frequently, the MiG pilots used this advantage to dive down, make one firing pass, then use the energy from their dives – and their superior engine thrust – to zoom back up out of reach. However, eventually they would have to return to base (RTB). If the Sabres were still "on station", they had to dive through the American fighters and "run for it", hoping to reach the sanctuary of the Yalu before their adversaries' superior dive performance and higher Mach limit resulted in the F-86s closing to machine gun range and opening fire.

F-86 Sabre and MiG-15 comparison specifications		
	F-86A-5	**MiG-15bis**
Powerplant	5,450lb thrust J47-GE-13	5,952lb thrust VK-1A
Dimensions		
Span	37ft 1in	33ft 1in
Length	37ft 6in	35ft 2in
Height	14ft 9in	12ft 1.67in
Wing Area	274 sq ft	221.75 sq ft
Weights		
Empty	10,093lb	7,998lb
Loaded	13,395lb	11,147lb
Thrust/Weight	0.45:1	0.60:1
Wing Loading	44.25lb/sq ft	45.0lb/sq ft
Performance		
Maximum Speed	679mph at Sea Level	669mph at Sea Level
Combat Radius	374 miles	240 miles
Initial Rate of Climb	7,300ft/min	9,060ft/min
Service Ceiling	47,600ft	50,840ft
Armament	6 x 0.50-cal. (12.7mm) Colt-Browning AN/M-3 machine guns	1 x N-37D 37mm and 2 x NR-23 23mm cannon
Gunsight	A-1C(M) radar-ranging	ASP-3N gyro; stadiametric ranging

THE STRATEGIC SITUATION

Opposite
By the time the two elite Soviet V-VS divisions were in place to defend "MiG Alley" the frontlines had stabilized in the vicinity of the 38th Parallel, and the ground war settled into a static, stalemated situation. The 4th FIG Sabres returned to the Korean Peninsula to challenge the MiGs' air defense of Communist supply lines in the rear areas, being reinforced by the 51st FIG in December 1951, and supplemented by RAAF Meteor F 8s and USAF F-84E Thunderjets at various times. Meanwhile, well behind Communist lines, the other V-VS units trained PLAAF and KPAF MiG-15 fighter divisions to assume a greater role in defending "MiG Alley" in subsequent years.

When the "Great Leader of the Korean People" Kim Il-Sung sent his KPA charging southwards across the 38th Parallel on June 25, 1950, it was a compact, but relatively powerful, force – ten infantry divisions supported by 90 T-34 tanks and an air division. The latter consisted of two operational air regiments which, according to recently released Russian archival documents, were equipped with 93 Ilyushin Il-10 *Shturmovik* "assault" (ground attack) aircraft and 79 Yakovlev Yak-9P fighters. These were improved versions of the standard Soviet propeller-driven combat types that served with the V-VS during the final days of World War II.

Kim Il-Sung's victory appeared assured. The Republic of Korea Army (ROKA) had only eight under-strength divisions of incompletely trained and lightly equipped troops and the Republic of Korea Air Force (ROKAF) just 16 training and liaison aircraft. However, US President Harry S. Truman was not going to allow the practically defenseless ROK to fall to Communist forces. He quickly ordered the US Far East Command, under Gen Douglas MacArthur, to intervene. The USAF's Japan-based Fifth Air Force F-80C Shooting Stars soon dominated the skies, achieving aerial superiority by the end of the first week. Augmented by propeller-driven NAA F-82G Twin Mustang night/all-weather interceptors and left-over World War II NAA F-51D Mustangs, American fighters had downed two-dozen North Korean aircraft by July 20, after which the KPAF withdrew from combat.

More critical to achieving air supremacy was the bludgeoning airfield attacks administered by FEAF Bomber Command Boeing B-29 Superfortresses and Fifth Air Force Douglas B-26B/C Invaders, supported by sporadic strikes by US Navy and

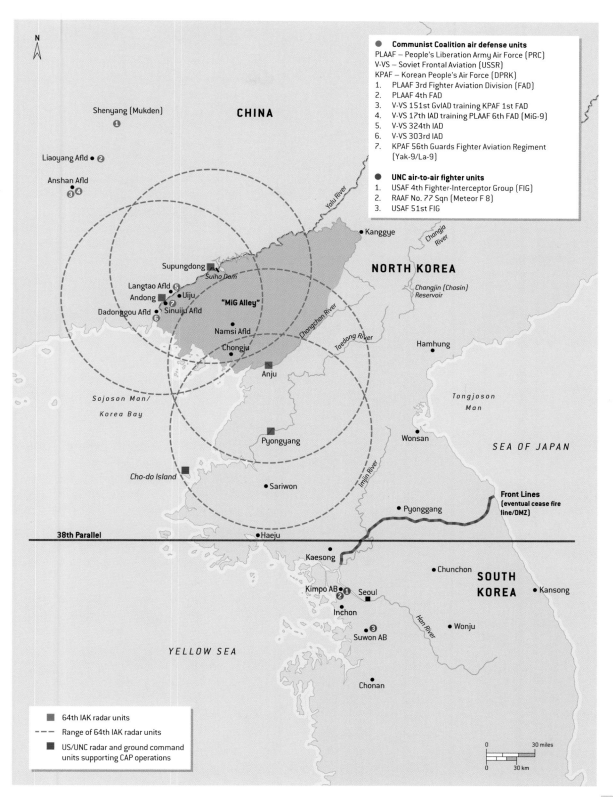

N

Communist Coalition air defense units
PLAAF – People's Liberation Army Air Force (PRC)
V-VS – Soviet Frontal Aviation (USSR)
KPAF – Korean People's Air Force (DPRK)
1. PLAAF 3rd Fighter Aviation Division (FAD)
2. PLAAF 4th FAD
3. V-VS 151st GvIAD training KPAF 1st FAD
4. V-VS 17th IAD training PLAAF 6th FAD (MiG-9)
5. V-VS 324th IAD
6. V-VS 303rd IAD
7. KPAF 56th Guards Fighter Aviation Regiment
   (Yak-9/La-9)

UNC air-to-air fighter units
1. USAF 4th Fighter-Interceptor Group (FIG)
2. RAAF No. 77 Sqn (Meteor F 8)
3. USAF 51st FIG

CHINA

Shenyang (Mukden)
①

Liaoyang Afld ● ②

Anshan Afld
③④

Supungdong
Suiho Dam

Langtao Afld ⑤
Andong ● ● Uiju
Dadonggou Afld ● ⑥ Sinuiju Afld
⑦

"MiG Alley"

Namsi Afld

Chongju

Kanggye

Changjia River

NORTH KOREA

Changjin (Chosin) Reservoir

Yalu River

Chongchon River

Taedong River

Hamhung

Anju

Sojoson Man/ Korea Bay

Tongjoson Man

Pyongyang

Wonsan

SEA OF JAPAN

Cho-do Island

Sariwon

Imjin River

Pyonggang

Front Lines (eventual cease fire line/DMZ)

38th Parallel

Haeju

Kaesong

Chunchon

SOUTH KOREA

Kansong

Kimpo AB ● ①
② Seoul
Inchon

③
Suwon AB

Wonju

Han River

YELLOW SEA

Chonan

■ 64th IAK radar units
- - - Range of 64th IAK radar units
■ US/UNC radar and ground command units supporting CAP operations

0 ___ 30 miles
0 ___ 30 km

In the first four weeks of the war, USAF Shooting Stars, Mustangs and Twin Mustangs swept the KPAF from the skies of Korea, shooting down 14 Yak fighters and ten Il-10 assault aircraft (one of which is seen here falling to an F-51D). After July 20, 1950, the KPAF was no longer seen over the frontlines. (NMUSAF)

The first Soviet MiG-15s in China were those of the elite 29th GvIAP, which deployed to Dachang airfield, near Shanghai, on 1 April 1950 to defend the port from KMT air attacks. After training PLAAF pilots on the type, the 29th GvIAP moved to Dalian, where it was issued with new MiG-15bis fighters. The regiment subsequently saw action over the Yalu from December 1950 to February 1951.

Royal Navy carrier-based attack aircraft. By late August FEAF Intelligence estimated that bombing raids and strafing fighters had destroyed 110 KPAF aircraft on the ground. Soviet sources tell us only 20 operational Il-10s and a solitary Yak-9P survived to be withdrawn into China.

The tide turned when US forces launched a surprise amphibious assault at Inchon on September 15. By the end of the month the North Koreans were in a pell-mell retreat northwards. Anticipating an unfavorable outcome once the Americans entered the war, Chinese Communist Chairman Mao Zedong ordered the 13th Army Group (twelve infantry and three artillery divisions) of the People's Liberation Army (PLA) – to prepare for defensive operations along the Yalu River. Three weeks later MacArthur's UNC forces crossed the 38th Parallel and began pushing deep into North Korea, determined to completely destroy the DPRK, reunite the peninsula as a free, democratic nation under ROK president Syngman Rhee and place US troops at China's door.

Unwilling to accept this eventuality, Mao began reinforcing what he now called the Chinese People's Volunteer Army (CPVA) and directed Gen Peng Dehuai to prepare for counter-offensive operations to turn the American-led UN forces away from the PRC's border with North Korea. The CPVA commanders argued that they needed air cover or else they would suffer debilitating losses to the UN air forces.

At this time the PLAAF's sole operational unit was the 4th Mixed Air Brigade, which had been established in June 1950. It consisted of (one regiment each of) 38 MiG-15s, 39 La-11 prop fighters, 39 Tu-2 bombers and 25 Il-10 ground attack aircraft. Training for the brigade's 126 pilots began in July, and by September 28, 31 of them had soloed in the MiG-15. Ten weeks of operational (combat) training commenced on October 1 in the Shanghai area under the tutelage of the V-VS's 106th IAD. Although the latter was designated a fighter aviation division, this was actually a combined unit consisting of the V-VS's premier MiG-15 regiment (the 29th GvIAP, transferred from the 324th IAD), a regiment of La-11 fighters and a mixed bomber/attack regiment with Il-10s and Tu-2s.

The 106th IAD had arrived in the Shanghai area in March 1950, and its fighter regiments began air defense operations on April 1, shooting down six KMT aircraft before its mission was changed to training the PLAAF on these types. Additionally, some 878 Russian personnel were busy training 1,911 student pilots using 180 Yak-11/18 trainers at seven PLAAF aviation schools, the first half graduating in October 1950.

Consequently, Mao appealed to Soviet Premier Josef Stalin to provide the air cover needed over the CPVA's troops and supply lines, as well as protect the rear areas. After prevaricating nervously, Stalin eventually promised "124 MiG-15" jet fighters to cover the Chinese troops. Initially, Maj Gen Ivan M. Belov's 151st GvIAD was deployed to Shenyang (called Mukden by the Russians) to train the PLAAF's 3rd and 4th Fighter Air Divisions (FADs) on the MiG-15, but this tasking was soon modified to include providing air cover "for the troops of the PLA's 13th Army Group, [but] will not fly across the state border with the Korean People's Democratic Republic".

The movement of V-VS MiG-15 units to the FEMD had already begun. Worried that US intervention in the Korean conflict might spread beyond the peninsula, the V-VS transferred Lt Gen Georgiy A. Lobov's 303rd IAD to the Primorye (formally the *Primorsky Krai*, or "Maritime Territory") region to guard the large Soviet naval base at Vladivostok in July 1950.

To provide similar protection for the PRC's primary naval base at Dalian (formerly the Imperial Russian Port Arthur), the V-VS transferred the personnel of the famous 177th IAP "Talalikhin regiment" from Lobov's unit to Xiansilipu airfield. The 177th was named after ace V. V. Talalikhin, who had become the V-VS's first Hero of the Soviet Union (HSU) in World War II after he rammed a German bomber at night over Moscow in August 1941. Once at Xiansilipu, the 177th was joined by the pilots of the 29th GvIAP and the staff of the 106th IAD, who arrived from Shanghai on October 3. One week later the new unit was designated the 50th IAD, issued with 80 brand-new MiG-15bis fighters and charged with the air defense of the Liaodong Peninsula.

Additionally, Stalin ordered an enlarged and accelerated training program to rapidly expand the PLAAF and prepare it to take over the responsibility of covering its own troops. Nine V-VS aviation divisions were sent to China for a year to train a similar number of PLAAF air divisions on MiG-9s, La-9s, Il-10s and Tu-2s.

The first class of graduating Chinese student pilots were assigned to the newly-formed PLAAF air divisions, which were attached to the newly-arrived V-VS combat units for a four-month conversion course to qualify them on their respective aircraft types. This was followed by a two-month operational training course to teach them formation flying, combat maneuvers and weapons employment. Once training was completed, the Soviet units' aircraft would be turned over to the just-trained PLAAF air division. The second PLAAF pilot training class, graduating in April 1951, would repeat this evolution. Thus Stalin hoped to quickly establish an effective Communist Chinese air force, thereby obviating the need for his own V-VS units to be thrust into a physical, and lethal, confrontation with the US that had potentially disastrous thermo-nuclear consequences.

On October 19 – the same day that UNC units entered the North Korean capital of Pyongyang – Mao ordered Peng's now heavily reinforced CPVA to cross the Yalu into North Korea, and six days later they began "spoiling attacks" (the first of four phases of offensive operations designed to conquer the Korean peninsula) against

It was the USAF's B-29 bombers and US Navy carrier-based attack aircraft destroying the town of Sinuiju and attempting to "drop" the two large bridges spanning the Yalu River that convinced the Soviet V-VS generals that their MiG-15 commitment to protecting these strategic structures must be increased. (US Navy)

ROKA forces. Consequently, MacArthur obtained Truman's approval to use FEAF's B-29s to destroy "every means of communication and every installation, factory, city and village" up to the Chinese border. Additionally, Fifth Air Force fighter-bombers began attacking Chinese units near Sinŭiju, just across the river from Andong (formerly Antung, now Dandong), China.

The only Communist air defense forces available were a reconstituted KPAF unit (the 56th Guards Fighter Aviation Regiment, which had originally been very involved in the initial KPA invasion, before being driven from the battlefront by Fifth Air Force fighters) of 24 Yak-9Ps and Belov's 151st GvIAD, which consisted of three MiG-15 regiments operating from Shenyang, Liaoyang, and Anshan airfields. These units were tasked with providing air cover for CPVA troops crossing the two massive 3,085ft (940m) long bridges into North Korea. The KPAF Yaks were quickly ravaged by USAF Mustangs, losing nearly half their number in air combat and airfield attacks, and were soon withdrawn. Consequently, it was up to Belov's MiGs to protect the bridges. Launched on sweeps over the river to keep the American fighter-bombers away, several formations had tentative combats with USAF Mustangs and Shooting Stars.

On November 8, FEAF sent 70 B-29s to destroy Sinŭiju and another nine against the two bridges. Some 584.5 tons of incendiaries razed the city, killing 2,000 civilians, and the southern approaches to the bridges were battered by 1,000lb HE bombs, but they still stood. The next day the US Navy also tried its hand at "dropping" the Sinŭiju bridges, using Douglas AD Skyraiders and Vought F4U Corsairs, escorted by Grumman F9F Panther jet fighters.

That day, Col Gen Stepan A. Krasovskiy, commander of all Soviet aviation units in the FEMD, Lt Gen Lobov and Maj Gen Belov were meeting in Andong to discuss with CPVA commanders how much Soviet assistance was required to ensure the air defense of northeast China. These discussions – together with personally seeing the destruction across the river and witnessing the dramatic air battles fought between Belov's MiGs and the US Navy raiders – convinced Krasovskiy that the Kremlin's restraints on MiG operations should be relaxed and that the commitment to provide an adequate air defense should be increased.

Over the next two days the MiG-15 proved itself to be a capable bomber destroyer. First, a pair of MiG-15s mortally damaged a USAF RB-29A reconnaissance aircraft checking on the condition of the two bridges. The Superfortress crashed attempting

Two of the 4th FIW's squadrons (49 F-86A-5s and 200 personnel) sailed across the Pacific aboard the former World War II escort carrier USS *Cape Esperance* (CVE-88). The random-looking parking arrangement of the jets in this photograph illustrates the hasty embarkation, while the variety of tail flashes attests to the collection of 36 of the very newest FY49 models from other FIWs so that the 4th was equipped with the very latest version of the F-86A. (John Henderson via Warren Thompson)

an emergency landing at Johnson AB, Japan, killing five crewmen. The next day MiGs shot down a B-29 bombing Uiju, just upstream from Sinŭiju. Five more Superfortresses were damaged by MiG cannon fire during the next three weeks.

The appearance of the MiG-15 in the skies of North Korea – but more critically, its destruction of the first B-29 – instantly energized the USAF to meet this dramatic increase in the severity of the Communist air threat. Previously reluctant to send America's best jet fighter to the theater – its obsolescent F-80C proved more than sufficient to dominate the KPAF's obsolete propeller-driven aircraft – the USAF had reserved its Sabres for the potential Cold War conflagration for which it was feared the Korean conflict was merely an initial diversionary campaign. However, the FEAF's bombers obviously needed protection from the new swept-wing nemesis.

Consequently, on the evening of the very first Superfortress loss, USAF Chief of Staff, Gen Hoyt S. Vandenberg, offered two wings of new jet fighters to the FEAF commander, Lt Gen George E. Stratemeyer, to counter the threat posed by the speedy MiG-15s. These were the 4th FIW, with its advanced F-86As, and the 27th Fighter Escort Wing (FEW), flying straight-wing Republic F-84E Thunderjets.

Just beyond the Yalu River, the Chinese rebuilt the former World War II Japanese Army Air Force airfield at Langtao (lower right), near Andong, with a jet-capable 6,000ft-long concrete runway and hard-surfaced taxiway in December 1950, and the brand new Dadonggou (upper left) airfield in May 1951. The Soviets based the 324th IAD at Langtao and the 303rd IAD at Dadonggou. (Dick Petercheff via Warren Thompson)

Three days later, the East Coast-based 4th FIW received its movement orders and hustled to gather up its personnel, aircraft and equipment to head west. Two squadrons flew to San Diego, California, to be loaded aboard former World War II escort carrier USS *Cape Esperance* (CVE-88), while the 336th FIS "Rocketeers" landed at McClellan AFB, California, from where its jets were barged to Oakland and loaded aboard four fast tankers as deck cargo. The tankers arrived in Japan first, and the 336th FIS had most of its Sabres flying by the time its sister squadrons arrived. On December 15, the "Rocketeers" flew seven Sabres to Kimpo AB to establish Det A of the 4th FIG, which would soon grow to 32 jets.

Meanwhile, on November 15, responding favorably to Krasovskiy's appeal, Stalin ordered the establishment of the 64th IAK, with Belov being promoted to lieutenant general to command it. The 64th was given a solitary mission to perform – provide air defense over the Yalu. Specifically, the new command was to "protect political, administrative and economic centers from air strikes and American aerial reconnaissance, as well as industrial objects, railroad junctions, bridges, force concentrations, the bridges over the Yalu River and electrical power stations in the Andong area".

Once the turbulence of hasty unit realignments subsided, the 64th IAK would consist of Lobov's 303rd IAD and the premier MiG-15 unit in the Soviet air force, the 324th IAD. Selected to lead this elite unit in battle was Col Ivan N Kozhedub, HSU three times over and the Allies' highest scoring World War II ace with 62 victories. The staff and its two regiments travelled by train to Dongfeng airfield, in Jilin Province, in mid-December, quickly assembled their MiGs and began three months of intense combat training in preparation for meeting the Americans over the Yalu.

But until these two crack units were ready, Col Aleksey V. Pashkevich's 50th IAD replaced the 151st GvIAD on the "frontlines", scoring its first victory on December 4 by shooting down a USAF jet-powered RB-45C reconnaissance aircraft over Anju, North Korea. And it was the 50th IAD that met Sabres of the 4th FIG in the first sporadic clashes over the Yalu later that month. In these the Russians lost three MiGs to the Americans' loss of one F-86 before the relentlessly advancing CPVA troops forced the 4th FIG's Det A to withdraw to Japan. During this period the 50th IAD lost a total of seven MiG-15s and five pilots. US records verify that in addition to the F-86A and RB-45C, an F-80C, an RF-80A and an F-84E were lost to MiG-15s from the 50th IAD between 4 December 1950 and 6 February 1951, when the division was withdrawn.

Following Peng's failed "fourth phase offensive", the Chinese drive stalled 60 miles south of Seoul. By March the CPVA had been pushed back north and the front stabilized more-or-less along the 38th Parallel. Now safe to return to Korea, the 4th FIG began flying its Combat Air Patrols (CAP) over the Yalu from Suwon AB, 24 miles south of Seoul. Early the following month Kozhedub's 324th IAD started mounting combat missions from Andong, and in May Lobov's 303rd IAD arrived in-theater. The stage was now set for the soon-to-be titanic struggle for air superiority over the Yalu.

THE COMBATANTS

USAF FIGHTER PILOT TRAINING

The majority of American pilots making up the 4th FIW were combat-experienced World War II veterans who had flown P-38s, P-47s and P-51s against Hitler's Luftwaffe in Europe and/or the Imperial Japanese air arms in the Pacific only five years before. However, the young lieutenants in the squadrons – as well as those who would be replacing them as the conflict dragged on – were recent graduates of the USAF's new post-World War II pilot training program.

Revised to include jet aircraft, this program consisted of two phases – basic training on the legendary NAA T-6 Texan and advanced training using the new Lockheed T-33 T-Bird derivative of the F-80C Shooting Star.

2Lt Richard B. Keener is a prime example of the USAF pilot training experience of the early 1950s. A year after graduating from college in Ohio, Dick Keener was accepted for flight training in the summer of 1951. Following two weeks of classroom instruction on "fundamentals of flight" and meteorology, Class 52-F began basic flying training, which initially consisted mostly of touch-and-go flights around the airport's traffic pattern. As Keener later recalled, "My first solo flight was on November 9th, and soon after we concentrated on instrument training, cross-country flights, aerobatics, night flying, etc. We were flying bright yellow 550hp T-6G trainers. My last flight in basic training was on March 21, 1952. Dual flying totaled 84 hours and solo totaled 46 hours, all in the T-6G. From there I was transferred to Williams AFB, Arizona, for advanced training and a chance to fly jets!"

At Williams AFB, there were two more weeks of academics awaiting the new arrivals, where they were instructed on high speed/high altitude flight and taught more advanced meteorology. Keener's experience in advanced training was that "there were three different aircraft types involved – an earlier model T-6, T-33 and F-80. The T-6D phase lasted two months, and involved formation, aerobatics, cross-country (including night flying) and instrument training. My first jet flight in a T-33 was on June 19, 1952. From that time on all of our flying was done in the T-33 or the F-80 Shooting Star. Of course the emphasis at that time was always on formation and cross-country flying. I logged 70 hours in the T-6D, 26 hours in the T-33 and 39 hours in the F-80".

Graduating on September 13, 1952, Keener received his pilot's wings with a total of 265 hours flying time. Afterwards, he reported to Nellis AFB for F-86 training, before being sent to Korea to fight the MiG-15s. His first flight at Nellis was a local check ride in a T-33, and that same day he soloed in the Sabre. Ten days later, Keener was fully checked out in the F-86A, and his fighter training focused on formation flying, cross-country, aerobatics, fighter-bomber and air-to-air combat tactics. For a pilot bound for Korea, the tactics segment was vital, involving bombing, strafing, firing at towed aerial targets and learning the combat tactics being used over "MiG Alley". When he completed his final flight at Nellis in December 1952, Keener had more than 80 hours in the F-86 Sabre.

1Lt Dick Keener, having completed pilot training and the "Fighter School", flew F-86 Sabres with the 335th FIS "Chiefs" out of Kimpo AB, Korea, in 1953. (Richard Keener via Warren Thompson)

SOVIET FIGHTER PILOT TRAINING

Likewise, the majority of pilots making up the Soviets' 303rd and 324th IADs were highly experienced World War II veterans with more than 300 hours in jet fighters. But unlike the Americans, who introduced fresh pilots into their Korean-based F-86 units before the combat veterans rotated home, thus providing a highly experienced cadre from whom new wingmen learned as they became operational in the frontline, the Soviets replaced their MiG-15 units by whole divisions. Once these two crack, but depleted, IADs transferred back to "Mother Russia" in February 1952, they were replaced with ones that had just completed conversion to the high performance, swept-wing MiG-15, and therefore had little experience in the jet, and none in combat.

Even worse for the Communists, as the 303rd and 324th IADs departed, the Chinese-led *Ob'yedinyennaya Vozdushnaya Armiya* (OVA or "Unified Air Army") was formed. This was made up of two PLAAF and one KPAF MiG-15 divisions, with the two new, inexperienced, IADs from the USSR's *Provito Vozdushnaya Oborona Strany* (Air Defence Troops of the Nation or *PVO-Strany*) attached to it "for their protection". This resulted in soaring victory tallies for the USAF Sabre pilots from the spring of 1952. In light of the losses suffered by the Communists, it is instructive to examine the pilot training program administered by the Soviets to prepare Chinese and Korean MiG-15 pilots to meet new "Sabre jocks" – such as Dick Keener – in combat over the Yalu.

Like its American equivalent, Soviet pilot training typically took about a year. But Stalin sought to minimize the USSR's exposure and risk in its involvement in Korea and wanted the PLAAF to assume responsibility for air operations within the year, so he ordered the V-VS to shorten its initial pilot training program to six months, followed by a "six-month aircraft conversion program to train them to employ Russian-made airplanes and combat techniques".

The Russians always sought a more equitable balance than the USAF between teaching the theoretical aspects of flying – aerodynamics, meteorology, navigation, flight physiology, etc. – and instructing its practical application. However, the Chinese 4th to 9th grade education levels of the pilot recruits and the language barrier proved almost insurmountable obstacles in teaching the "peasant soldiers" the complex concepts upon which modern military aviation is based. Even with translators and

KPAF MiG-15 pilot Lt No Kum-Sok dressed in his flying gear. Note that he lacks an anti-G-suit. (NMUSAF)

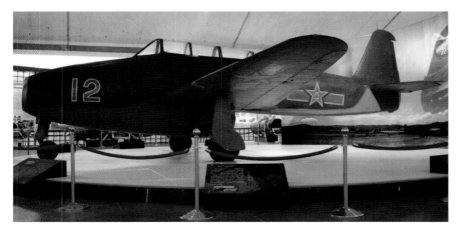

Each Soviet MiG-15 regiment included two Yak-17UTI fighter trainers within its ranks – the only two-seat jet trainer in the V-VS inventory at the time. Four hours of dual instruction was provided using these straight-wing jets before the PLAAF or KPAF student was allowed to fly the single-seat MiG-15. (Mark Pasqualino)

former KMT aviators assisting each classroom session, it took almost twice as long to teach any subject. Consequently, "the standards of instruction were lowered, and the course of theoretical studies was abbreviated".

The V-VS's post-World War II flying training program had two phases – elementary training in the Yak-18 light trainer and basic training in the more robust Yak-11, the 700hp equivalent of the NAA Texan. Typically, a Soviet student graduated with 150-180 hours flying time in total, but in the abbreviated program administered to the PLAAF, Chinese students averaged 27 hours on the Yak-18 and 30 on the Yak-11.

When the first class graduated in October 1950, some 120 new pilots were assigned to the first three PLAAF MiG-15-equipped fighter air divisions (the 2nd, 3rd and 4th FADs, with a similar number forming MiG-9 FADs). Instruction began with academic courses on "the design, defects and natural effects" of jet aircraft (16 hours), the design and operation of jet engines (20 hours), radio equipment (six hours) and oxygen equipment (12 hours), and the practical study of the aircraft's cockpit and controls (24 hours).

Each academic day included seven hours of instruction, phased to align with the practical (flight) training. The flying training began with three additional hours in the Yak-11. Called "clean up", this was to ascertain the student's proficiency, and led directly to four hours of dual instruction in the two-seat, straight-wing Yak-17UTI jet trainer. Finally, the student soloed on the MiG-15, amassing some 16 hours in type before graduating.

By the time a PLAAF MiG-15 pilot completed training, he had a mere 80 hours of flight time, of which only 20 were in jet aircraft. Patently inadequate, there were more than 100 fatal accidents in the first half of 1951 alone. Moreover this training "covered nothing of combat group harmony (called 'formation integrity' in the West), let alone the fact that nothing was learned about combat flight tactics".

USAF F-86 FIGHTER TACTICS

The tactics used by all the successful air forces during and after World War II were those originally pioneered by the Luftwaffe in the early stages of that conflict and perfected in the crucible of combat. Consequently, in Korea, the basic fighting formation used by both sides was the classic four-aircraft "fingertip" formation, called a "four-ship" by the Americans or a *zveno* ("flight") by the Russians – two pairs (called "elements" or *pary*, respectively) working together, each element/*para* comprising a "shooter" and a "cover" fighter.

Offensive fighters of the early 1950s primarily had two missions – fighter sweep (or patrol/CAP), called *frei jagd* ("free hunting") by the Luftwaffe, and close escort. Typically, the 4th FIG launched squadron-strength (three "four-ship") patrols to sweep the MiGs from the "Alley", and thus enable the fighter-bombers to accomplish their interdiction missions. Close escort was used in an attempt to protect the much slower World War II-era B-29 bombers, but this was generally disdained as being overly restrictive, limiting the Sabre pilots' freedom of action by having to maintain visual contact and stay relatively close to their charges.

Although this photograph is posed (fighter pilots never wear their hats in a real mission briefing), the briefing board the aviators are looking at is real, showing a typical F-86 fighter sweep formation. "Red Flight" is in the lead, "Blue Flight" is offset "down sun" and "Yellow Flight" (covering) is positioned "up sun" to intercept any MiGs that might attempt to interfere with the mission by attacking the other flights. (Richard Becker via Warren Thompson)

USAF fighter training continuously improved, keeping pace with the changes in tactics in Korea. By contrast, Soviet units, due to the secret nature of the USSR's involvement and the insular nature of their various commands, had no "cross-tell" to acquaint new arrivals with operational issues, making their "learning curve" extremely costly in terms of the number of jets lost and pilots killed. The USAF's jet fighter tactics were first codified by double-ace "Boots" Blesse in his seminal, and classified, publication *No Guts, No Glory!* of March 1955. (Author's Collection)

Following more than two years of combat in Korea, ten-victory ace Frederick "Boots" Blesse codified the USAF's Sabre tactics in the classified confidential *"No Guts, No Glory!"* instruction manual he wrote as the F-86 training squadron (3596th Combat Crew Training Squadron) commander at the Nellis "Fighter School" in 1955.

For attacking an enemy formation with a four-ship, "the lead F-86 element should attack the enemy element farthest back [in their formation]. As the second enemy element breaks into the attack, they will probably go down so that they can get help from the lead enemy element. The lead F-86 element then switches the attack, if possible, to the lead enemy element, in which case the second F-86 element stays high and fast and watches for the possible return of the enemy second element.

"If it is not possible to switch elements when the initial bounce is made, then the lead F-86 element [leader] should press his attack on the second enemy element until [the wingman calls out] the need to counter any action taken by the lead enemy element. Any time the lead F-86 element is attacked and the second element has an advantage over the attacker, the second element [leader] should exploit this advantage, even though it may require a permanent separation of the two F-86 elements.

"Sometimes, committing both elements to the offensive immediately, with an interval of seven to ten seconds between attacking elements, will be productive. By having both enemy elements engaged, you almost cut out the possibility of mutual support between enemy elements."

FIGURE A

The basic F-86 fighting formation was the "four-ship" composed of two pairs or "elements", each with a leader – who was designated the "shooter" – and a wingman who provided visual lookout of the element's vulnerable "six o'clock". The leading (left-hand) element in this view has assumed the "fighting formation" in preparation for attacking an adversary, the wingman having moved from his normally wider "patrol position" to about 200ft from his leader – closing until he could read the "tail number" on his leader's vertical fin – approximately 35° off his leader's tail. The second element is shown in the "patrol formation", where the all-round visual lookout of both pilots is enhanced by the wingman flying approximately 300ft out to the side, 55° off his leader's tail – a position determined by the ability to read the "FU-number" on the side of his leader's empennage.

FIGURE B

The "four-ships" of Sabres provided a "layered defense" to protect UN fighter-bombers from the MiG-15s. The MiGs were generally able to climb above the "contrail level" (typically 36,000-42,000ft) before the UN formations arrived, so the leading F-86s – commonly "Red Flight" – would approach immediately beneath that visually-revealing altitude band, normally at 35,000ft. "Blue Flight" would be positioned to one side of the leaders, stacked at 25,000ft. "Yellow Flight" would be on the opposite side, stepped down at 20,000ft, as the last layer of defense for the fighter-bombers, who generally flew in the "upper teens" or trailed in the "low twenties" as they ingressed to the target area.

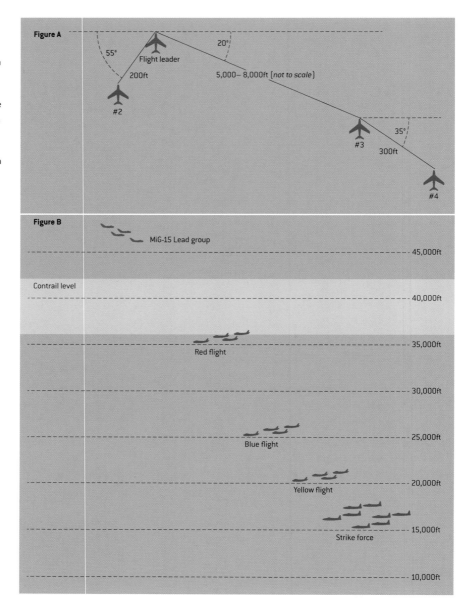

Frequently, however, because the MiGs normally had an initial height advantage, the Sabres had to survive the first attack before "going offensive". "Assuming the attack is on the high [second] F-86 element, and is discovered normally, the second F-86 element [leader] should nose down to pick up speed, calling out the bandits to the flight leader as he does so. The lead F-86 element waits for an opportune moment to turn hard into the attack. The second F-86 element should, if at all possible, turn away from the lead element [giving them room to turn in on the attackers] as long as doing so does not give the attackers any advantage.

"If the initial attack is on the lead element, the second element should come down immediately and attempt to parry the attack. If the attack is broken up, the second

F-86 element should continue to follow up any advantages gained by pressing home the attack on the first enemy element.

"Look around! Don't let the other enemy element surprise you. A radio call will be necessary to advise the lead element that they are clear at present, but on their own from this time on."

Once split up, Blesse advised the element leader to "turn into the attackers when they are just outside firing range (2,500-3,500ft). Fight as though you are a single until you get an advantage by overshooting the attackers and reversing on them as they slide past the tail. If the attackers make the turn and you end up with them at your airspeed at 'six o'clock', spread out [your wingman so that] if they stay together and attack one of you, the other can swing back in, sandwiching them between you and your wingman. If, as you spread out, one of them slides out so each of you has an attacker, each of you must forget the other and do whatever is necessary to shake your attacker. If one gets free, naturally, attempt to help the other."

SOVIET MiG-15 FIGHTER TACTICS

Defensively, 1950s fighters' primary mission was to protect specific targets – such as cities, industrial complexes, hydro-electric powerplants and airfields – from enemy air attack. Soviet V-VS doctrine was to intercept incoming air raids approximately 68 miles (100-120km) from the anticipated target, thus allowing adequate time/distance to destroy most of the approaching force, or cause them to jettison their bombloads and turn for home.

To provide early warning, the Pegmantit 3M (P-3M, M for "mobile") VHF-band radar was deployed to Andong. The original 1947 model *PVO-Strany* P-3A had a range of 80 miles (130km), but the V-VS's truck-mounted variant proved effective only out to 56-72 miles (90-115km), resulting in inadequate warning of approaching UNC air raids. Indigenously developed from data published by the Massachusetts Institute of Technology Radiation Laboratory, the P-3 was the third iteration – and first operational example – of Soviet early warning radar. The P-3's low power output restricted its range, it could not detect targets "flying among the hills" and its crude Gonimeter height-finding equipment was limited to 10,000m (32,808ft) altitude.

When radar operators from the 64th IAK detected approaching UNC formations, the SKP scrambled the alert flights. With the MiG-15's tremendous rate-of-climb, the Soviet pilots were able to zoom up through the "contrail layer" to a "perch" position above the Sabre's ingress altitude, giving them an initial positional advantage. (NMUSAF)

Despite these drawbacks, in 1951 the 64th IAK deployed four radar-equipped auxiliary command posts (called a *Vynosnyy Punkt Upravleniya* or VPU) and eight visual reporting posts into North Korea. These provided early warning and ground control intercept (GCI) coverage approximately 170 miles (250-300km) south-southeast of the Yalu River.

The Soviets employed two types of fighter interception – scrambles from an alert readiness posture or a sweep, called *svobodnyy okhot* ("free hunt") by the Russians – down the anticipated approach course of the enemy. Normally, each division began the day with one regiment at Readiness No. 1 (pilots and groundcrew immediately available near their aircraft in the reveted parking area), and a second with two squadrons at Readiness No. 1 and the third at Readiness No. 2 (aircraft manned and parked on hardstands next to the runway end).

When given the scramble order by the *Startovaya Komandnyy Punkt* (SKP or "starting command post"), the squadron at Readiness No. 2 would start engines, turn onto the runway and takeoff in pairs 12-15 seconds apart, the entire squadron being airborne in two minutes. If the regiment's other squadrons were ordered off simultaneously, the first *zveno* would taxi to the end of the runway in about two minutes time and the last would be airborne 2.5-3 minutes later, resulting in the regiment launching 24 MiG-15s in less than five minutes. The pilots would take one turn to join up in their combat formation, and after climbing to their operational altitude on the north side of the Yalu, they would be vectored by GCI, with a height advantage, towards the approaching enemy.

While this was the primary mode of operations, "the most successful solution for covering rear area objectives [to be defended] was achieved by the use of fighter patrols along the most probable routes of approach by the enemy aircraft". This was done by launching one regiment as the "lead group" to initially disrupt the incoming raid and "tie up" the escorts, while two or three regiments formed the "strike group" to engage

OPPOSITE

FIGURE A

The basic MiG-15 fighting formation was the *zveno* or "four-ship", composed of two pairs, each with a leader who was responsible for the forward hemisphere and a wingman responsible for the rear hemisphere. When actively searching for the enemy, such as when flying as part of the "Lead Group" or as the "Cover Group" protecting the "Strike Group", the two pairs would be spread approximately 1,200ft (350m) apart so as to allow both element leaders to search the skies ahead. Each wingman flew about 20° back from line abreast, offset approximately 425ft (125m) to allow him to visually clear the leader's "six o'clock", but remain close enough to attack a target with him. If the whole formation was to attack a single target, the second pair would fall into trail with the lead pair.

FIGURE B

A maximum response to a large enemy raid approaching called for both IADs to launch four regiments, with the fifth held in reserve. In the vanguard of the attack would be the "Lead Group", with a high formation to engage the F-86 escorts and a low formation to intercept and disrupt the enemy fighter-bombers by forcing them to jettison their drop tanks and, hopefully, their ordnance. Approximately four to eight minutes behind (two to three minutes if the incoming raid was discovered late) would be the "Strike Group", composed of a main body to destroy the incoming raiders and a cover group to protect them from enemy escorts. As these groups disengaged and began to return to home, the "Reserve Group" would be launched to intercept any F-86s trailing the MiG-15s to their bases. In this depiction, each MiG-15 symbol represents one *zveno* of four fighters.

FIGURE C

After the two elite V-VS fighter divisions were replaced by inexperienced and poorly trained PVO, PLAAF and KPAF units, losses mounted, so stronger formations were needed to effectively counter the standard USAF "four-ship" of Sabres. The six-ship "wedge formation" was used from the end of 1952 onwards, the two "wing" pairs flying approximately 1,150ft (350m) higher than the leading pair, both offset about 40° to either side of the formation leader's tail. The second pair trailed about 1,800ft (550m) behind the leader and the third pair a little further back, allowing the second pair to fly between themselves and the leaders during heavy maneuvering, and a little further to the outside of the formation, allowing the formation leader's wingman freedom to maneuver to that side.

Figure A

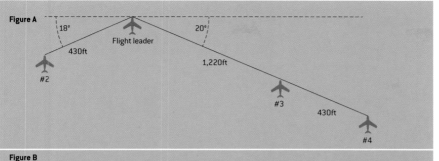

Figure B

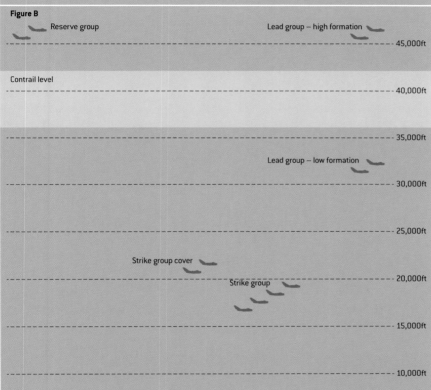

Reserve group

Lead group – high formation

45,000ft

Contrail level

40,000ft

35,000ft

Lead group – low formation

30,000ft

25,000ft

Strike group cover

Strike group

20,000ft

15,000ft

10,000ft

Figure C

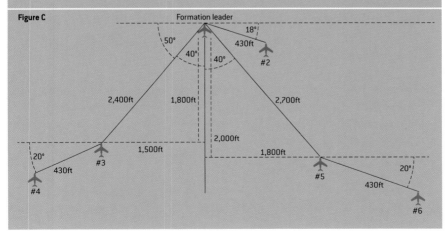

GEORGE L. JONES

Born in New York on May 12, 1918, George Jones grew up in Florida and graduated from the University of Florida in 1940, joining the US Army as a 2nd Lieutenant immediately afterwards. His infatuation with flying initially led him to become an air observer in the 97th Observation Squadron, based at Miami, Florida, but this failed to satisfy his hunger to be a pilot. Accepted into USAAF pilot training in November 1942, Jones graduated high in his class the following May, and was selected as an instructor pilot in P-47 Thunderbolts. With his expertise in the cockpit increasing, his star rose rapidly. In September 1944 he became a P-47 flight commander in the 76th Training Wing at Seymour Johnson AAF base, North Carolina. Joining the co-located 301st FW in February 1945, Jones transferred to the Pacific, where he flew long-range P-47Ns escorting B-29 Superfortresses attacking Japan.

Following World War II, Jones briefly commanded a squadron in the 51st FG on Okinawa until the unit converted to F-80As. Although eager to get into jets, he had to do one more stint in propeller-driven fighters, commanding the 96th FS flying P-51H Mustangs from Grenier AFB, New Hampshire, until September 1949. Jones' chance finally came when he was named the Operations Officer in the famous 56th FIG at Selfridge AFB, flying F-80s until the unit converted to the Sabre in early 1950. He subsequently joined the 4th FIG in Korea, where he was placed in command of the 334th FIS "Fighting Eagles" in June 1951. Four months later he was named Deputy Commander of the 4th FIG, and was spot promoted to Colonel. By year-end Jones had become the Commander of the 51st FIG, which had just converted from F-80Cs to the new F-86E. During his combat tour in Korea, he became the USAF's 30th jet ace, finishing his tour with 6.5 aerial victories, all MiG-15s.

Lt Col George L. Jones, as commander of the 334th FIS "Fighting Eagles" in Korea. (Author's Collection)

Following the Korean War, Jones commanded the 3595th Training Group at Nellis AFB, and the 15th Tactical Fighter Wing at MacDill AFB, Florida, flying various jet fighters before retiring as a Colonel on June 6, 1968. During his career Jones was awarded the Silver Star, Bronze Star and two Distinguished Flying Crosses. Col George L. Jones died on February 18, 1997.

and destroy the raiders. The lead group, which may have been scrambled using the previously-mentioned procedure, was followed four to eight minutes later (or just two to three minutes if the raid was discovered very close to its target) by the strike group. Another regiment or two would form the command reserve, which would launch 10-15 minutes afterwards to cover the return of the lead and strike groups and intercept any enemy fighters following them to their bases.

Like the Americans, the Russians fought as four-ships, or *zvena*, which could break into pairs, or *pary*, for individual combats. The V-VS history of the Korean War stressed "the superiority of the MiG-15bis gave it the ability to carry out active

SERGEI M. KRAMARENKO

Born in a Ukrainian village on April 23, 1923, Sergei Kramarenko grew up on a *kolkhoz* (collective farm) near the Volga River. He realized his childhood dreams of becoming a pilot by volunteering for flying training at the Dzerzhinskiy aeroclub, near Moscow, his standing in the upper part of his class leading to military flight training from April 1941.

Graduating as a sergeant pilot, Kramarenko first saw action flying the LaGG-3 with the 303rd IAD's 523rd IAP over Stalingrad in November 1942. During the winter he achieved his first victory while flying the La-5, shooting down Fw 190A-3 Wk-Nr 2265 of Oberfeldwebel Karl Stadeck. The latter, from 2./JG 51 "Mölders", was killed in the combat. After recovering from burns and injuries suffered when he was himself shot down by a Bf 110, Kramarenko joined the crack 176th GvIAP. Flying frequently on the wing of Maj Ivan Kozhedub, the USSR's leading ace, he proved to be an excellent wingman, being credited with ten shared victories. Kramarenko was credited with his second solo success, another Fw 190, on April 16, 1945.

Remaining with the 176th GvIAP during the post-war period, Kramarenko's first jet was the Yak-15, and in 1949 he and his regiment transitioned to the MiG-15. Deploying to China in October 1950 with his division, now led by Col Kozhedub, Kramarenko eventually commanded his regiment's 3rd *Eskadra*. During his combat tour he was credited with 13 victories (two Meteor F 8s, two F-80s and nine F-86s) and was shot down once, in January 1952, by a Sabre just minutes after claiming another F-86 destroyed. Kramarenko was awarded the *Zolotaya Svezda* of the *Geroy Sovietskogo Soyuza* (Golden Star of the HSU) on November 10, 1951 for his tally of kills.

Following the Korean War, Kramarenko rose rapidly through the ranks, attending the prestigious Monino Air

Promoted to Lieutenant Colonel as a result of his Korean War exploits, Sergei Kramarenko was selected to attend the prestigious Monino Academy in 1954. (via Igor Sejdov)

Force Academy, commanding the MiG-17-equipped 167th GvIAP in Georgia and serving as air defense advisor to the Iraqi and Algerian air forces. Promoted to Major General, Kramareko finally retired in 1977 and currently resides in Moscow.

combat against superior numbers of enemy fighters, but also to break off combat in disadvantageous situations, using its superiority in vertical maneuver to seek a more advantageous position. [In] air combat between the MiG-15 and F-86, the former strove to use its better vertical speed and maneuver, which would support combat at all altitudes. The basic flight maneuvers used by the MiG-15 in combat included the combat turn [often called a "chandelle" – 40-50° banking climb followed by a "wingover" and turning descent], the tightening [defensive] spiral, the zoom climb and the 'split-S'. When carrying out these maneuvers, in all cases it was necessary to have a reserve of speed."

COMBAT

Once Peng Dehuai's "fourth phase offensive" spent itself, the battle lines ebbed northwards. The runway at Suwon AB was repaired, and on March 5, 1951 the 4th FIW Sabres returned to Korea with the deployment of the 334th FIS "Fighting Eagles". During that month encounters in "MiG Alley" were sporadic due to the extreme range for the Sabres and the reduced strength of the 151st GvIAD – one MiG-15bis was lost to an F-86 on March 24 (but no victory was credited by the USAF), with the Sabres losing none. During this period (February-March 1951) the 151st GvIAD also lost four MiGs in combat with USAF F-80Cs – two in a mid-air collision, one in a collision with an F-80C and one shot down by an F-80C.

At the beginning of April the elite 324th IAD replaced the 151st, the latter returning to Anshan to instruct PLAAF and KPAF pilots.

Kozhedub's 324th launched its first mission from Langtao on April 3, and the MiG-15 pilots quickly learned that they had met their match in the 4th FIG's Sabres. Crossing the Yalu still climbing for altitude, the Soviet aviators were attacked by a mixed formation led by 335th FIS "Chiefs" commander, Lt Col Benjamin H. Emmert Jr, a six-victory ace from the Mediterranean theater in World War II. One MiG-15 was shot down, its pilot being killed in action (KIA), and two others crash-landed, damaged beyond repair (DBR). Emmert was credited with one victory, as were Capt James Jabara (the first of 15 kills for the future 334th FIS ace) and two lieutenants. One F-86 was lost due to fuel exhaustion, its pilot becoming a prisoner of war (PoW).

As Capt Sergei Kramarenko, deputy commander of the 176th IAP's 3rd *Eskadra*, later recalled, "All in all, the result of this action turned out quite sad – we'd lost a pilot and three machines. The event showed us clearly that one shouldn't engage the Sabres without providing oneself with an advantage in speed and altitude. Doing otherwise

Sabres returned to "MiG Alley" in March 1951, initially operating from Suwon AB. Here, an element of the 336th FIS "Rocketeers" takes off from the base's primitive PSP runway for their 245-mile flight to the patrol area. (NMUSAF)

meant putting oneself under the fire of the Sabres' machine guns. When they had the advantage in both speed and altitude [the Sabres] would have complete freedom of action and attack, and strike at our airplanes with ease!"

Rebuffed in their challenge to the 4th FIG's air superiority, Kozhedub focused instead on repulsing the FEAF B-29 raids that were dropping one bridge after another into the Yalu River. The largest air battle thus far occurred over Sinŭiju on April 12, when MiG-15s intercepted 39 Superfortresses that were being escorted by 54 F-84s (from the 27th FEW) flying close escort. The bombers also had "top cover" provided by 24 Sabres (from the 334th and 336th FISs) led by 4th FIG commander Col John C. Meyer, a World War II ace with 37.5 victories to his name and the future commander of Strategic Air Command.

Once Soviet GCI radars spotted the incoming bombers, Kozhedub scrambled three waves of MiGs – the first two of 14 jets each, five minutes apart, followed 23 minutes later by another dozen. The first two waves were quick to climb to a height above the escorting Sabres, then dove through them to engage the bombers in high-speed "slashing" cannon attacks. The F-86s followed them through the bomber formations, straining past "red-line" to get within machine gun range while being shot at by B-29 gunners and F-84s alike!

Sabre pilots were credited with four MiGs shot down – by Meyer, Jabara (his third) and two other flight leaders. Actually, Kozhedub lost no fighters, although five jets returned to Langtao damaged. On the other hand, the MiG-15s' 37mm and 23mm cannon proved devastating to the American bombers. Three B-29s were shot down, a fourth crashed on landing and four more were damaged to a lesser extent.

Convincingly proving its capabilities as a bomber destroyer, the early model MiG-15s accounted for six B-29s lost in April. However, it was less effective as a fighter, losing eight aircraft (with two pilots killed and two more wounded) for the one F-86 lost to fuel starvation.

The MiG-15 excelled as a bomber destroyer, accounting for six B-29s lost in April. Here, one is seen chasing a Tu-4 "Bull" – the Soviet clone of the B-29 – during training. (FoxbatFiles.com)

Obviously the F-86A-5 was clearly superior to the early model MiG-15, so Kozhedub traded his surviving examples for the 151st GvIAD's improved MiG-15bis version, receiving 47 of these at the end of April. The following month he obtained a further 16 jets directly from the Novosibirsk factory. At the end of May, Maj Gen Lobov's three-regiment 303rd IAD began arriving at the just-finished airfield at Dadonggou (also called Tatung-kao and Miaogou by the Russians). The regiment's commitment to combat in Korea now meant that there were 153 MiG-15bis to challenge the 44 F-86As based at Suwon.

En route to "MiG Alley". Eight 335th FIS Sabres cruise north just below the "contrail level" on May 20, 1951. The nearest F-86A (FU-327) is being flown by Capt James Jabara (334th FIS), who would claim his fifth and sixth victories on this very mission, officially making him the USAF's first jet ace. (James Dennison via Warren Thompson)

ENGAGING THE ENEMY

Once the Sabre pilot had successfully maneuvered to the "six o'clock" of the enemy, it was time to close in for "the kill". With the A-1C(M) gunsight's wingspan adjustment dial (fig. 1) set to 35ft (approximating that of the MiG-15) and the AN/APG-30 radar locked onto the target (red light (fig. 2) illuminated), the gunsight "pipper" showed where the 0.50-cal. "bullet stream" would be at that range (under current G). The reticle (a ring of ten dots on the windscreen and gunsight's combining glass) would equal the wingspan of the target at that range (fig. 3). When the reticle turned red, the range was less than the number selected in the sight range dial (fig. 4) on the left side of the gunsight. At that point, the pilot maneuvered smoothly to hold the "pipper" on the target, waited 0.5-1.0 second for the ballistics to be computed (or "stabilized") and then opened fire, with accuracy assured.

Should the radar be inoperative (as it often was) the reticle diameter would conform to the wingspan of the target (set on the wingspan adjustment dial (fig. 1)) at the range selected in the sight range dial (fig. 4), and the "pipper" would indicate the position of the "bullet stream" at that range under current G. The Sabre pilot would

close until the wingspan of the target equalled the diameter of the reticle, and when the "pipper" was placed on the target and allowed to "settle" ("stabilize"), accurate firing could commence. As the Sabre closed in range, the pilot would twist the throttle grip clockwise to maintain the reticle diameter to match the target's wingspan, thus sending a corrected range signal to the gunsight, which then adjusted the "pipper's" depression to the new range.

If multiple targets were present and the radar locked onto one not being engaged, the pilot could "step" the radar to the target in the reticle by pressing the radar target-reject button (fig. 5) on the control stick. If engaging a target below 6,000ft AGL, the radar would lock onto the ground, providing grossly inaccurate range information to the gunsight. In this case the pilot would press the "sight stiffen" button (fig. 6) atop the throttle to position the "pipper" at a range of 850ft. If the Sabre pilot was trailing the MiG at greater range, he would have to position the "pipper" a commensurate distance ahead of the target (known as "pulling lead") or close to within 1,000ft for the "pipper" to accurately predict the location of the "bullet stream" at that range.

"CASEY JONES"

The stage was set for a major effort in June, one in which the Soviets attempted to obtain air superiority over the Chinese supply lines to support Peng's planned "sixth phase offensive". Realizing that the CPVA could not overwhelm the UNC forces with manpower alone, the aim of this phase was to recover DPRK territory north of the 38th Parallel that had been lost to the UNC's spring counter-offensives. Peng's previous campaign ended prematurely on May 20, having been defeated, according to his personal report to Mao, by ravaging UNC air attacks on his logistics system. Only 60-70 per cent of the needed supplies – food, water, clothing, ammunition and other equipment – reached the frontline troops as a result.

With the Chinese clamoring for increased air cover over their supply lines from the Yalu to Pyongyang, the 64th IAK challenged the 4th FIG repeatedly during the third week of June. By this time the combat experience of the Soviet pilots began to show in an increased aggressiveness, improved combat proficiency and heightened confidence over what they had displayed in the past. Tactics had matured to where almost every *zveno* was protected by a *para* covering formation. This led the Sabre pilots (and USAF Intelligence) to believe that the covering fighters were Russian instructors directing Chinese students (the *zveno*), and they began referring to the *para* as "honchos" (Japanese for "boss").

The red-nosed MiGs of the 324th IAD were particularly visible, and thinking these were the personal markings of one or two senior Russian instructors, the covering flight leader was frequently called "Casey Jones" (a legendary aggressive American locomotive engineer). His wide-flying wingman was rarely seen, leading the Americans to believe that "Casey Jones" primarily operated solo.

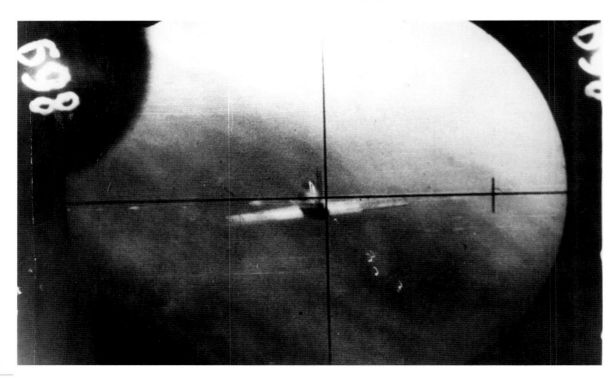

"Casey Jones'" view of Lt Col Glenn Eagleston's Sabre. Although not Kramarenko's gun camera film, this was his perspective as his 23mm cannon shells (in this case indicated by the squiggly lines passing beneath the right wing of the F-86) severely damaged the USAF fighter.

According to the 336th FIS "Rocketeers" CO, Lt Col Bruce Hinton (who had scored the first MiG kill of the Korean War when he shot down Maj Yakov Efromeenko of the 29th GvIAP on December 17, 1950 – the Soviet pilot ejected safely), "Ol' Casey, also known as 'Honcho', was an exceptional pilot. His normal procedure was to sit up high all by himself, then dive down at a very high rate and attack any F-86 that seemed isolated and alone. He was easily spotted in the air since his MiG had a significant paint job, with a red nose and fuselage stripes [*sic*]".

On June 17, in the first battle of this series, "Casey Jones" turned out to be Capt Sergei Kramarenko. On his second mission that day the Soviet pilot led a flight of six MiG-15bis that had been sent aloft to intercept a dozen Sabres flying in two formations. The first clash proved inconclusive, with Kramarenko ducking into a cloud deck to escape being "sandwiched" between the Sabres' main group and the covering four-ship. Turning and climbing back out of the clouds, Kramarenko found himself alone, above and behind the Sabres' covering flight.

As he later recalled, "Now, below me, there were these three Sabres, which were looking for me below them. Without losing not even a second, I jumped them. Now it was my turn to attack, but somehow they spotted me and immediately they split – the wingmen performed a diving turn to the left, and the leader a climbing right turn. This tactic was a trap, for whichever one I attacked, I would be forced to turn my tail to the others and then they would get me under fire. I [had to] decide fast. Who shall I attack? Should I attack the pair which was diving, or the Sabre which was climbing? If I jumped the first ones, the latter would dive after me and he would shoot me down. That's why I choose the latter. So, I dived and soon I put myself behind him. I aimed, and at a distance of about 600m [1,970ft] I opened up.

"To slow down and hold my fire until I was closer to the Sabres was impossible, because the two remaining jets could catch me. My shells struck the Sabre. Evidently, some of the projectiles hit it close to the engine, because the aircraft began to leave a trail of dark gray smoke. The Sabre began to descend, and later entered into a steep dive. I did not see my victim fall, because when I looked back I saw a couple of Sabres at 500m. I immediately reversed my heading, passed over the Sabres and dived to the right towards the [Suiho Dam] hydro-electric station on the Yalu River. I hoped that the gunners of [its anti-aircraft] batteries would help me to get these Sabres off of my tail. And that was what happened."

During the course of this engagement Lt Col Hinton had spotted the Sabre of Lt Col Glenn Eagleston (an 18.5-victory World War II ace who was now CO of the 334th FIS), adding "and he wasn't alone! About 500ft behind him was a MiG with a red nose and stripes on his fuselage. 'Casey Jones'! And he was pounding the Sabre with cannon fire. I could see the MiG fire, and see its shells hitting the Sabre, with flame and sparks marking the strikes on the fuselage".

Hinton's account correlates well with Kramarenko's, ending with "[the MiG] suddenly broke away and dove toward the Yalu, easily pulling away from me. I broke off and looked for the stricken F-86. I found him sort of floating at about 20,000ft. The fires had gone out, but he had some big holes in the fuselage. I tried talking to him, but his radio had been hit by another cannon shell. We were flying at about 0.7 Mach, and he was steadily losing altitude. It took forever, but we finally made it to friendly territory. I called Suwon tower, informing them that I was bringing in a

MiG-15bis COCKPIT

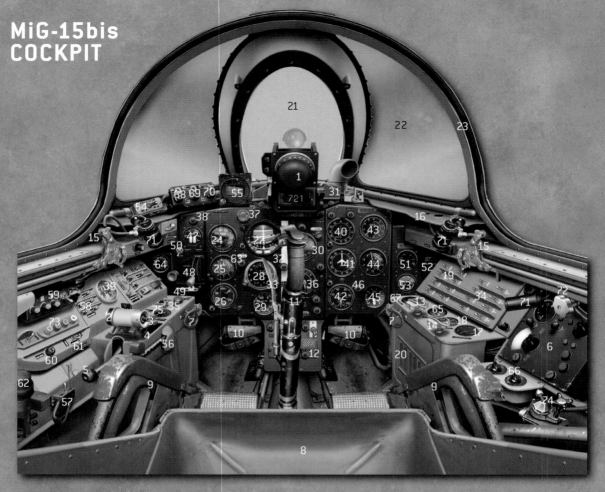

1. ASP-3N gunsight with crash cushion
2. Throttle
3. Push-to-talk radio button
4. Aileron boost selector
5. Flap selector lever
6. ARK-5 radio compass tuning panel
7. Emergency canopy jettison (both sides of cockpit)
8. Cartridge-fired ejection seat
9. Ejection handles (both sides of seat)
10. Rudder pedals
11. Control column with gun, air brake and ordnance/tank jettison buttons
12. Ordnance control panel
13. Emergency landing gear valve
14. Emergency flap valve
15. Canopy locks (both sides of the cockpit)
16. Windscreen de-mist and ventilation
17. Main pneumatic pressure gauge
18. Main hydraulic pressure gauge
19. Master switches

20. Pneumatic and hydraulic access panel
21. Bullet-proof windscreen
22. Side-light transparency
23. Canopy sealing hose
24. KUS-1200 airspeed indicator
25. VD-17 altimeter
26. RV-2 radio altimeter
27. AGI-1 attitude/turn-and-bank indicator
28. Clock
29. M-0.95 Mach meter
30. VAR-75 vertical speed indicator
31. Gunsight reticule adjustment knob
32. White stripe for positioning control column in spin recovery
33. Pneumatic brakes 'bicycle' control lever
34. "Russian accordion" electrical switch panel
35. Fire warning light and fire extinguisher button
36. KES-857 fuel quantity gauge
37. Landing gear not down warning light
38. Flaps down light

39. Brake pressure gauge
40. ARK-5 radio compass ADF indicator
41. DGMK-3 gyro compass indicator
42. EMI-3P fuel and oil pressure/temperature indicators
43. TE-15 engine tachometer
44. TGZ-47 jetpipe temperature gauge
45. EM-10M low pressure fuel gauge
46. Gyro-compass "align to north" button
47. Pilot's oxygen flow indicator
48. Landing gear control handle
49. Landing gear position indicators
50. Landing light switch
51. VA-340 volt/ampere meter
52. Pitot tube heater switch
53. Cockpit differential pressure indicator
54. Homing Far/Near switch
55. Magnetic compass
56. Throttle locking lever
57. ARK-5 radio power switch
58. Three-range toggle switches – radio compass

59. RSI-6K VHF radio control panel
60. Air brake indicator light
61. Air brake toggle switch
62. Pilot's oxygen regulator
63. Mach 0.92 warning light
64. Oxygen pressure gauge
65. Emergency flap air pressure gauge
66. Ultra-violet light rheostat (x2)
67. Emergency landing gear pressure gauge
68. Gun cocking button – 23mm cannon inner
69. Gun cocking button – 23mm cannon outer
70. Gun cocking button – 37mm cannon
71. Ultra-violet cockpit lights (both sides of cockpit)
72. Air emergency valve
73. EKSR-46 signal discharger firing buttons
74. Cockpit pressurization selector
75. Aileron booster system pressure gauge

cripple, and to clear the runway and alert the meat wagon and fire trucks. He was going to have to make a wheels-up landing as the MiG had shot out all the controls". Following the successful belly landing, the Sabre's riddled hulk was cannibalized for parts and used as a decoy at the end of the runway – although DBR on June 17, F-86A-5 49-1281 was not written off for a further eight days.

The June air battles continued throughout the week, and although the challenge to the Sabres' superiority was serious, it was met effectively, albeit with increased losses. The 64th IAK suffered seven MiG-15s destroyed and four pilots killed, while the 4th FIG lost four Sabres (including Eagleston's) and three pilots KIA. Despite these successes, the Communists realized that Belov's two MiG divisions had not wrested air superiority from the Sabres, so Stalin – unwilling to commit any more Soviet fighter units to the contest – urged Mao to send "at least eight fighter aviation divisions" into combat, and provided 372 MiG-15s to replace the MiG-9s in six PLAAF FADs to do so. He emphasised that "it is necessary for the Chinese to rely only on their own aviation at the front". The PLAAF promised to have these forces ready for battle in November. Meanwhile, Peng canceled his "sixth phase offensive".

"GABBY" ARRIVES

The summer's monsoon season blanketed Korea in bad weather – cloud bases at about 2,000ft (600m), layered up to 32,500ft (10,000m) most days – with morning fog and incessant rain effectively grounding the 64th IAK and limiting all-jet combat to just six engagements. The 4th FIG continued to dominate, destroying ten MiGs and killing four pilots for only two combat losses (one of which was again due to fuel exhaustion, with both pilots okay). Early in this period the 4th FIG was reinforced with the arrival of 30 more F-86A-5s and 45 new F-86E-5s (17 Sabres had been lost to all causes thus far) and a large cache of spare parts. The latter allowed the maintenance technicians to take advantage of the reduced operational tempo to get as many Sabres as possible ready to meet the increased numbers of MiGs.

Along with the new F-86s came a score of fresh, eager and experienced fighter pilots. These were led by the flamboyant Col Francis S. Gabreski, the third-ranking and top living USAAF ace from World War II with 28 victories over the Luftwaffe. "Gabby" Gabreski was the commander of the 56th FIG at Selfridge AFB until he was named as the 4th FIW's deputy commander, and he sailed to Korea with a group of 56th FIG pilots he had hand-picked to accompany him back into battle. "Gabby" scored his first MiG kill on July 8.

The results of Kramarenko's fire – 23mm cannon shells damaged Eagleston's Sabre (FU-281) so severely that he had to belly-land the jet back at Kimpo. DBR, the jet was written off a week later after all useable components had been cannibalized to help maintain other F-86s. (John Henderson via Warren Thompson)

Improved weather conditions in September allowed RF-80 photo-reconnaissance missions to resume, and FEAF Intelligence was surprised to find that the Communists had taken advantage of the weather-related reprieve to begin building three new airfields in North Korea. Halfway between the Yalu and Pyongyang, a clutch of three air bases – Namsi, Taechon and Saamcham – were rapidly being completed, and FEAF Bomber Command hurried to destroy them.

Once again, the MiG-15 proved its mettle as a bomber destroyer. On October 23, nine B-29s (of the 307th BG) headed for Namsi airfield, escorted by 55 F-84s (49th and 136th FBGs) and screened by 34 Sabres. The 303rd IAD's three regiments scrambled 58 MiG-15bis, followed 15 minutes later by 26 from the 324th IAD's two regiments. The 18th GvIAP led the assault, with two squadrons engaging the Sabres and the third attacking the bombers. The MiGs shot down three B-29s and badly damaged five others, two of which made emergency landings at Kimpo and were later "transferred to depot for disposition" (USAF bureaucratic double-speak for DBR). In spite of claims from bomber gunners, Thunderjets and Sabres, no MiGs were lost, and only three were damaged in the battle.

After losing eight bombers destroyed and five damaged during the month, FEAF HQ ordered that daytime bomber operations be discontinued from October 28. This was a tacit admission that the Fifth Air Force had failed to achieve air superiority north of the

The highest-scoring surviving USAAF ace of World War II, Col "Gabby" Gabreski (right) returned to combat in the summer of 1951 and got his second MiG kill on September 2 that year. One week later he congratulated the USAF's second and third jet aces, 1Lts Dick Becker and Ralph "Hoot" Gibson. (Richard Becker via Warren Thompson)

On October 22, 1951, the MiG-15 once again proved deadly as a bomber destroyer when three of them mortally damaged one of nine B-29s targeting Taechon airfield. Seen here from one of the other Superfortresses in the formation, the jets are peeling away following their firing passes. (Harry Ruch via Warren Thompson)

Chongchon River sufficient to allow the B-29s to do their job, and that these ponderously slow World War II bombers were not survivable against modern swept-wing jet interceptors. This victory came at some cost to the Communists, however, as eight MiG-15bis and three pilots had been lost to Sabres during this period.

In November the 64th IAK was joined by two PLAAF and one KPAF MiG-15 divisions, organized into what was called the "1st United Air Army" (or OVA by the Soviets) and commanded by Chinese Gen Liu Zhen. This brought the total number of MiGs in the theater to 525, of which 290 were based in the Andong area once Takushan airfield – another 7,000ft concrete runway jet base 50 miles down the coast west of Andong – was completed. The rest were stationed at more distant Manchurian bases, except for the KPAF's 1st FAD, which deployed 26 MiG-15s to Uiju, in North Korea, on November 7.

Control of these increased forces was fractured since neither Mao nor Stalin would allow their units to be under the authority of the other. Consequently, while a separate OVA/KP (command post) was established only 60 yards from the 64th IAK/KP at Andong, coordination consisted only of the OVA HQ passing information to the Soviets so that the latter could time their launches to cover the withdrawal and return of Chinese and Korean fighters.

Responding to the MiG build-up in Manchuria and grievous losses to the B-29 force, HQ USAF dispatched 75 new F-86Es to Korea – enough to replace the 4th FIG's F-86A losses and establish a second unit, the 51st FIG, at Suwon. Compared with the first transoceanic shipment, this one was much better organized, as attested by the tidy parking arrangements aboard *Cape Esperance*. (James Hardin via Warren Thompson)

The introduction of PLAAF and KPAF units to the conflict more than compensated numerically for the departure of the V-VS's 151st GvIAD, which had completed its year-long mission and returned to the USSR (passing its MiG-15s to the KPAF). At the same time Gen Belov also departed, turning command over to Lt Gen Lobov, a HSU and 19-victory ace from World War II.

As more and more MiG-15s arrived in-theater, Sabre numbers grew to match the increased threat. The day of the slaughter of the FEAF B-29s over Namsi – known as "Black Tuesday" – Gen Vandenberg ordered that 75 more F-86E-1s, hastily gathered from various Air Defense Command units, be sent to Korea. Shipped in two batches, 36 jets went to the 4th FIG at Kimpo. Their mid-November arrival coincided with the movement of the group's third squadron from Japan to its Korean base. The remaining 39 went to Suwon, where the 51st FIG was ordered to transition from its war-weary Shooting Stars. This gave the Fifth Air Force 165 Sabres, with 127 of them based in Korea.

DOGFIGHTING A "HONCHO"

While the PLAAF and KPAF took a more active role in challenging the Sabres in "MiG Alley", the V-VS did not relent in its own efforts. On November 2, Lt Col George L. Jones, deputy commander of the 4th FIG, led 12 F-86As from the 334th FIS as escorts for two formations of F-84E fighter-bombers targeting rail yards and supply dumps near the Yalu. The Sabres were stacked in their typical tactical formation, with Jones leading "Red Flight" ingressing at 35,000ft. As he later recalled, "We were timing it to meet up with the fighter-bombers about half way to the target, and move ahead of them so that we would be on station before they arrived just in case there were MiGs waiting for them".

F-86A-5 COCKPIT

1. Windscreen and gunsight combining glass
2. A-1C(M) gunsight range dial
3. Gunsight wingspan adjustment dial
4. Radar on-target indicator light
5. Gunsight reticle dimmer control
6. Engine fire warning lights
7. Drop tanks pressure shutoff valve
8. Ammunition compartment heat controls
9. Cockpit pressure and temperature controls
10. Flight controls power and trim switches
11. Emergency speed brake control lever
12. Throttle
13. Speed brake control switch
14. A-1C(M) gunsight stiffen button
15. Microphone button
16. Flap lever
17. Bomb/rocket/tanks jettison button
18. Oxygen regulator indicators and controls
19. Landing gear handle
20. Landing light switches
21. Landing gear position lights
22. Parking brake handle
23. Low fuel pressure warning lights
24. Accelerometer
25. Voltmeter
26. Horizontal stabilizer position indicator
27. Exhaust gas temperature indicator
28. Cockpit air temperature indicator
29. Standby magnetic compass
30. Radio compass indicator
31. Airspeed indicator
32. Slaved gyro magnetic compass
33. Attitude indicator
34. Engine tachometer
35. Cabin pressure altimeter
36. Machmeter
37. Altimeter
38. Turn-and-slip indicator
39. Rate-of-climb indicator
40. Fuel flow meter
41. Fuel quantity gauge
42. Electrical system warning lights
43. Generator load meter
44. Clock
45. Free air temperature gauge
46. Oil temperature gauge
47. Fuel pressure gauge
48. Oil pressure gauge
49. Gunsight selection controls
50. Guns control switches
51. Bomb/rocket control switches
52. Bomb/rocket release interval control
53. Bombs control switches (behind control column)
54. Instrument panel light controls (behind control column)
55. Rudder pedals
56. Emergency hydraulic hand pump
57. Generator switch
58. Engine master switch
59. Engine start switch
60. Emergency ignition switch
61. Voltage regulator rheostat
62. AN/ARC-3 command radio control panel
63. AN/ARN-6 radio compass control panel
64. Hydraulic open-center system pressure gauge
65. IFF control panel
66. Hydraulic system pressure gauge
67. Ejection seat handgrips and triggers (both sides)
68. Control column
69. Horizontal stabilizer and aileron trim control
70. Radar target selector button
71. Bomb-rocket release button
72. Canopy emergency release
73. Emergency hydraulic selector
74. Pilot seat
75. Oxygen flow indicator
76. Oxygen pressure gauge
77. Landing gear emergency up button
78. Fluorescent light (both sides of cockpit)
79. Map case

The first strike group was greeted only by intense anti-aircraft artillery (AAA) fire, but as the second group of Thunderjets began their egress from the target area, "All of a sudden, 16 MiG-15s in loose trail formation appeared, and it couldn't have come at a worse time! I had just sent 'Red 3' and 'Red 4' back to base because they were very low on fuel. Now there were only two of us left in 'Red Flight'. I signaled my wingman [1Lt Richard Pincoski] to follow me down, and we dived right into the middle of the enemy formation. They started turning and twisting violently to get out of the way. They were shooting and we were shooting when suddenly they pulled up and zoomed for altitude.

"Out of the corner of my eye, I noticed one F-84 that had been cut off from his flight, and the MiG-15 leader was closing in on him for the kill – there was no way an F-84 could outrun a MiG. Both of these aircraft were about 5,000ft below us. I immediately rolled over and dived down at full throttle toward the pursuer, hoping to distract him before he could begin firing on his quarry. I fired a burst from far out of range with this in mind, as I closed on him. Apparently the MiG pilot saw my tracers because he whipped his airplane up to the right, climbing at full throttle. In the meantime, the F-84 made a fast and safe exit from the area while I closed on the MiG.

"I knew I had to fire quickly and hope for a lucky hit to slow him down before my airspeed bled off. I knew that as soon as the speed dropped, the MiG would zoom up and out of range. Suddenly, the MiG pilot slackened his turn. I put the sight on his fuselage and got a good lead and fired. My rounds missed, as I saw them go right under his belly. He tightened his turn again and I put the sight on him again and fired

Lt Col Jones' wingman's view of the chase. Although not Pincoski's gun camera film, this frame illustrates the relationship of the two Sabres in "hot pursuit" of the MiG. When the trigger on the F-86's control stick grip was pressed to the first detent, the gun camera was turned on – pressing to the stop fired the guns. The wingman here is not shooting bullets past his leader to get the MiG, he's just filming it. (Larry Davis)

– another near miss. I could not believe what was happening, and then it dawned on me exactly what he was doing. He was skidding in his turn, which meant his aircraft was not going where his nose was pointing.

"This time, I compensated a little since I knew he was skidding and pulled the trigger. The six 0.50-cal. guns roared as I held the trigger down. The sight was spectacular, like a high voltage line grounding on a piece of metal. The sparks were coming off his wing, fuselage and tail. I was completely engrossed in this, and suddenly the roar from my guns went silent – I was out of ammunition! The MiG was still flying as if it had not been hit at all.

"I called on my wingman to swing in and finish him off, and as he pulled in, I called for 'Red 2' to get closer. I swung out and checked all around and there were no other MiGs in sight. So 'Red 2' closed and started firing. His first long burst missed. The MiG was in a diving turn, skidding and jinking, and I radioed for my wingman to get even closer before firing. His second burst hit the MiG dead center as it made a dash for safety north of the Yalu River. He fired again and then ran out of ammo. There we were, both completely fired out!

"I knew I was riding a tiger, a Russian 'Honcho'. I told 'Red 2' that I was not going to let him get away, and to move out of my way. I flashed by my wingman, and with all the holes and metal fragments sticking out of the MiG's wing and fuselage, he had picked up a lot of drag, causing his airspeed to slow considerably. I figured that my overtake speed was in excess of 100 knots. The MiG pilot was watching my closure rate, and to avoid me he pushed over into a steep dive. Instantly, his fighter snap-rolled to the left. That did it! Evidently, the damaged airframe could not take the stress and something broke. 'Red 2' called out that the pilot had bailed out. I watched the empty MiG go straight down into the ground 15,000ft below me."

Jones and Pincoski shared this victory. Shortly thereafter Jones joined Gabreski in converting the 51st FIW to become the Fifth Air Force's second F-86 unit. Originally a three-squadron F-80C wing, the 51st FIG was now out-classed, flying obsolete Shooting Stars in an increasingly high-threat arena. With the F-84Es shouldering the burden of the air-to-ground war and the urgent need for more F-86s, the 51st was

The arrival of the 51st FIG's two F-86E squadrons at Suwon nearly doubled the Fifth Air Force's air-to-air combat power. Here, the 25th FIS jets, having just returned from an uneventful MiG sweep (note no gunpowder residue on the muzzle ports and the drop tanks still in place on the underwing pylons) get refueled while the pilots complete their aircraft maintenance forms. (Henry Buttelmann via Warren Thompson)

the natural choice to become the second Sabre wing. The conversion was accomplished without even "standing down" – according to one pilot, "we made the transition from F-80C to F-86E so fast the engines never shut down".

Initially, Gabreski's wing consisted of only the 16th and 25th FISs, and was manned by a few veteran F-80C pilots and a lot of brand-new "jet-jockeys" that had just converted from propeller-driven aircraft. As none of these aviators had had tactical training in the F-86, Gabreski brought with him a dozen of his former 56th FIG pilots from the 4th FIG in order to rapidly season his new unit.

"HONCHOS" GO HOME

Just as America's Sabre force was expanding in strength and increasing in skill, the Soviet contribution to the Korean air war began diminishing. At the end of January 1952, the newly-trained 97th IAD replaced the war-weary 324th IAD at Langtao, the survivors of the latter's ten-month combat tour departing for Mother Russia. Two weeks later at nearby Dadonggou, the equally inexperienced 190th IAD replaced the 303rd IAD, allowing the latter's veterans to also return home.

With their departure, the most important chapter in the 64th IAK's contribution to the Korea War came to an end. The divisions had battled the best and had decisively defeated FEAF's outdated B-29 force. Claiming an exaggerated number of UNC aircraft destroyed, including an inflated number of F-86s, the two divisions produced 39 aces and 18 HSUs. According to Soviet records, the 324th and the 303rd lost 56 MiGs, 49 of them to F-86s, and 32 pilots were killed. During this same period 35 Sabres were lost in combat with these units.

The two new IADs were from the *PVO-Strany*, the Soviet Union's independent air defense force. Their pilots were mostly brand-new to the MiG-15bis (only 20 per cent of them were World War II veterans, and none had flown in Korea), having just completed initial training. Few had more than 50 hours on type. Additionally, the

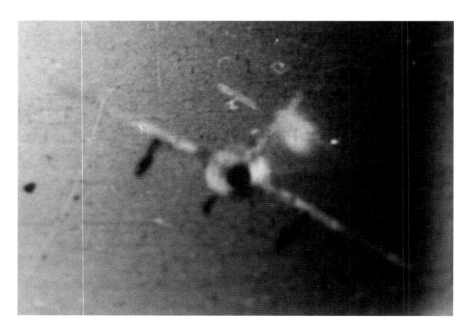

Taking advantage of FEAF HQ's "hot pursuit" exception, Gabreski's 51st FIW Sabres soon began "hawking" the Andong complex airfields – they shot down 26 MiGs on takeoff or final approach during May-July 1952. Gabreski called these operations "Maple Specials" because the "kills [were] as sweet as maple syrup". (Larry Davis)

Russian penchant for balanced – theoretical (academic) versus practical (flying) training – resulted in a skewed impression of their potential. The two units were selected because they "had received the best training marks from the supreme military authorities and were deemed ready for combat".

Being dedicated air defense units, their training concentrated on instrument flying, GCI procedures and attacking bomber formations, not air-to-air combat with enemy fighters. Kramarenko reported that when discussing his replacements with their squadron commander, "I ask[ed] him how well the pilots have been drilled. In response he said, 'Fine. All of them are first class pilots and can fly day or night in all weather.' I am surprised by this, and say, 'You need to practice aerobatics and battle maneuvers in pairs and flights as soon as possible.'"

The lack of proper combat training and the pilots' wholesale inexperience showed themselves immediately. In their first two months the divisions lost 27 MiGs (with a further 62 damaged) and ten pilots. In the same period only four F-86s were lost to MiGs, plus one to fuel starvation – three pilots were KIA and one MIA.

The situation worsened when FEAF HQ relaxed the rule forbidding F-86 flights into Chinese airspace – now it was allowed, provided the pursuer was in a position to complete the destruction of the enemy fighter. The aggressive American Sabre pilots quickly took advantage of the "hot pursuit" exception, and began actively CAPing – called "hawking" – the Andong airfields. The Soviets called these "airfield blockading" operations. The inexperienced Communist pilots were at a serious disadvantage as the MiG-15's low-altitude performance was inferior to the Sabre's, resulting in alarming losses. In the next two months the two IADs lost another 34 MiGs (and ten pilots), 17 of them being shot down either taking off or landing. Although not supported by the numbers, the perception, according to Soviet veteran Nikolay Ivanov, was that "No pilot survived such attacks".

This demoralizing situation prompted Lobov to withdraw one regiment from each division to rear-area airfields. Their mission was to provide defensive CAPs over their division's forward base to permit the unit's other regiments to get airborne safely. Additionally, the Soviets brought in the 133rd IAD, but this did little to improve the strength of the MiG-15 force because Col Aleksandr Shevtsov's 97th IAD had proven so ill-prepared that it was withdrawn for further training after only four months of operations.

Acknowledging the tactical soundness of this politically incorrect initiative, FEAF HQ used the same approach – with appropriate high-level approval – on June 23 to cover the massive USAF/US Navy strike flown against the Suiho Dam's Supung hydro-electric powerplant, right on the Yalu River. Built by the Japanese before World War II, this facility produced 300,000KW of electricity (half of it going to Chinese industries in Manchuria), and it was one of the sites the 64th IAK was specifically ordered to protect.

Sixty Sabres swept ahead of the first strike group (35 US Navy Skyraiders, with 35 F9F Panthers for flak suppression), 20 of them crossing the Yalu to "hawk" the four airfields now comprising the Andong complex. Consequently, no MiGs took off from these airfields. Additionally, the rear area bases were "socked in" with bad weather, grounding the MiG regiments there. Unopposed, 79 F-84Es and 45 F-80Cs followed, escorted by 24 more F-86s – the massive strike was devastatingly effective.

Even the Soviet Navy's MiG-15 units (one of which is seen here during a pre-mission flightline briefing) got into the fight. The *PVO-Strany* regiments experienced such high attrition and "combat fatigue" that pilots from the *Morskaya Aviatsiya's* 578th IAP were brought in to fly the 133rd IAD's MiG-15bis. After six months they were replaced by the navy's 781st IAP. (FoxbatFiles.com)

The last major air battle with the Soviet MiG-15s occurred – as fate would have it – on American Independence Day, the 4th of July. The 190th IAD launched 50 MiG-15bis in an attempt to counter a pre-strike sweep, but when the large formation of Thunderjets showed up on radar, GCI vectored the 494th IAP to intercept them. The Sabres engaged with an altitude advantage and, according to Soviet records, 11 MiG-15s were shot down, marking the single largest daily loss during the Soviet participation in the war. Two Sabres were downed in return, one pilot being KIA.

By the end of July the 190th IAD had lost 47 MiGs and the division's pilots "were near breaking point, and had begun to evade combat duty". Of the 154 pilots normally assigned to a *PVO-Strany* division, only 48 remained "combat ready". Most of the rest were medically grounded, the majority for chronic "battle fatigue". Consequently, the 190th IAD was also withdrawn from operations. It was replaced by the 216th IAD.

In an attempt to boost pilot numbers in-theater, the 133rd IAD was reinforced with personnel from the *Morskaya Aviatsiya's* (Soviet Naval Aviation) 578th IAP. Finally, at the end of August, the 32nd IAD arrived at Anshan to provide dedicated defensive coverage for the Andong airfields. This brought the Soviet contingent to 303 MiG-15bis (including 30 "nightfighters"), but from this point on Soviet participation in the air war gradually, but steadily, devolved to a token effort.

Once Stalin died on March 5, 1953, the Kremlin allowed Mao Zedong and Kim Il-Sung to reopen the ceasefire negotiations at Panmunjom and began withdrawing 40 per cent of its MiG force. According to Ivanov, after learning this, Soviet pilots "tended to be evasive in their encounters with enemy airplanes to avoid casualties" because "no one wanted to be the last to be killed in action".

USAF SABRES VERSUS CHINESE MiGS

The combined PLAAF/KPAF 1st UAA began fully fledged combat operations in November 1951, and initially "could only engage in air defense operations alongside the Russians". Following Mao's edict, the PLAAF's purpose was "to gain live combat experience", accepting that "there will be some losses in combat". By this time the Chinese had three combat-ready MiG-15 FADs, with four more becoming operational early in 1952. These rotated their regiments through the Andong complex airfields after each had experienced "five to seven large-scale air battles".

By the end of May all seven of these had flown combat missions in Korea, initiating some 447 pilots. It was good that the PLAAF's command accepted that losses would be incurred, because they were indeed high – of 294 MiG-15s assigned to these units, the PLAAF units had 75 destroyed and 27 damaged. In fact losses were so alarming that in June Mao suspended all combat missions for a month to review their operations.

While the obscenely low individual flying experience was a major cause of the huge disparity in PLAAF versus USAF losses, another major factor was that the Chinese FADs were still flying the older version of the MiG-15 that they had inherited from their V-VS instructor units, while the two Sabre wings (both now up to full three-squadron strength) had begun to receive the vastly improved F-86F.

In July 1952 the PLAAF assumed control of the Communist side of the air war, rotating six (later ten) MiG-15 FARs through the Andong complex airfields from their Manchurian rear area bases. Here, a Chinese FAR prepares to launch a training mission from one of the latter. (Tim Callaway Collection)

PREVIOUS
In a major modification designed to increase the lethality of the Sabre's armament, NAA fitted a quartet of Mauser-designed T-160 20mm cannon into ten F-86F-2 test aircraft in place of their six 0.50-cal. machine guns. The USAF sent eight of these aircraft to the FEAF for combat evaluation under Project *GUNVAL* (Gun Evaluation). After initial difficulties, in March 1953 the *GUNVAL* detachment scored four victories while flying with the 335th FIS at Kimpo AB. On the 29th Lt Col George Jones led Maj Wendall Brady in a two-ship sweep ahead of two-dozen F-86s, hoping that the Communists would focus on the much larger radar return trailing them. They did, sending eight PLAAF MiG-15s to engage. Jones spotted them, turned in behind the sixth MiG and while Brady kept the wingman at bay, blasted the target with a 92-round burst. The Chinese pilot ejected immediately and Jones had to barrel roll to prevent ingesting flaming debris. This was Jones' fifth confirmed victory, making him the USAF's 30th ace of the Korean War.

The new F-model was powered by the uprated J47-GE-27 engine producing 5,970lbs of thrust, the extra boost propelling it to the MiGs' operating altitudes. This allowed American pilots to now meet their adversaries at their "perch", effectively neutralizing the Communists' initial advantage. Later versions of the "Fox" – and 50 retrofit kits for the FEAF's initial batches – had a wing redesigned for high altitude, high-speed combat. Discarding the F-86A/E's automatic slats for a "hard" leading edge, its "6-3 wing" had a larger area, giving the F-86F a wing-loading superior to the MiG-15bis. At a combat weight of 12,585lbs, the "6-3 wing's" 302.3sq ft area gave the modified F-86F a wing loading of 40.1lbs/sq ft – approximately a ten per cent advantage over the MiG-15bis's 45lbs/sq ft. Now, not only could the Sabre "jocks" get to the MiGs' altitude, they could maneuver with them there as well.

Realizing that they were operating inferior fighters, the Chinese pressed their Soviet allies for the MiG-15bis at the end of May. In August, 267 uprated versions were provided, with the conversion of all seven FADs being completed by October. "Technical equality with the F-86s" had been restored.

Following the *PVO-Strany* defeat on the 4th of July and the PLAAF reassessment of its operations, that same month the 1st UAA formally took the lead in the Communist air effort by "conduct[ing] increasingly independent operations" and "carry[ing] out sustained operations involving a large number of air force units". The PLAAF placed four FADs on the "frontlines" at Andong (initially these were the experienced 3rd and 12th FADs with MiG-15bis to take on the Sabres and the brand-new 17th and 18th FADs to attack fighter-bombers with the older original version MiG-15), with a fifth based at Dongfeng specifically for the defense of the Supung hydro-electric plant. The KPAF's 2nd FAD also joined the command, the Soviets now being relegated to a minor supporting role.

This continued to be an expensive enterprise – rotating each division to Andong for a three-month period cost the units ten to fifteen jets each time, resulting in a request before the end of the year for 154 more MiG-15bis to keep these units at full

The F-86F provided a significant performance upgrade to the Fifth Air Force's Sabre units, allowing them to finally match, or best, the MiG-15bis. The F-model's "6-3 wing" had greater area, generating better turning performance at high speed/high altitude. The modification also increased the sweep slightly, necessitating a small "fence" on the wing leading edge. (NMUSAF)

strength. This attrition had a deleterious effect on the pilot force as well, the PLAAF increasingly sending "inadequately trained replacement pilots to frontline units".

On the other side, USAF/UNC Sabre strength only grew. In addition to re-equipping the 4th and 51st FIGs with the F-86F, by early 1953 sufficient numbers of the fighter-bomber-capable versions of the jet were arriving for the Fifth Air Force to re-equip two of its FBGs. The 8th converted from very war-weary Mustangs in January and the 18th transitioned from its equally tired F-80Cs in February. South African Air Force and ROKAF Mustang units also received Sabres at this point. The increased number of F-86s in-theater virtually neutralized the MiGs' previously

While USAF units were being upgraded throughout the conflict, Communist air forces "soldiered on" with the increasingly dated MiG-15bis. Because of its pervasive secrecy, there are very few photographs of Soviet MiG-15s in Korea. This is one of a 351st IAP "nightfighter" being prepared for a sortie at Langtao airfield. (Tim Callaway Collection)

The F-86F also provided an enhanced ground attack capability, with examples of the aircraft soon being issued to the 8th (seen here) and 18th FBGs. Flying the high-performance Sabres, fighter-bomber pilots could now "hold their own" against the previously predatory Communist jet menace, releasing the FIGs to concentrate on "killing MiGs". (Joe Lynch via Warren Thompson)

enjoyed ability to occasionally disrupt UNC fighter-bomber missions. By the time the truce went into effect the command had 132 F-86 fighter-bombers in Korea, powerfully augmenting its 165 Sabre interceptors.

By this time the dominance of the F-86 had become decisive. In 1953 the PLAAF lost 84 MiG-15s and the Soviets 47. During the same period the USAF lost 19 F-86s in combat with MiGs. May was particularly destructive, the Chinese losing 27 MiGs in combat with Sabres, prompting yet another operations review to investigate the causes of these "appallingly high casualties". One unit that was badly affected was the 12th FAD, which lost 48 of its original 60 pilots in a year of combat in Korea. By the time the PLAAF had fully addressed the causes of its grievous loss rate to the Sabre units, the ceasefire had come into effect.

STATISTICS AND ANALYSIS

The discerning reader will have noted by now that, except when mentioning individual pilot scores, this account does not reference "kill claims". This is because ever since modern high-speed aerial combat began in May 1940, due to the tremendous psychological stresses felt by pilots in battle "kill claims" have invariably been exaggerated. Historically, "kill claims" do not relate to the numbers of enemy aircraft destroyed, but instead only serve to underscore the intensity of the air battle. Any attempt to use "kill claims" to compute a "kill ratio", therefore, is grossly fallacious arithmetic.

Similarly, "victory credits" awarded by air arms are more closely related to political ends, propaganda grist and individual pilot glory. For example, in addition to the inherent flaws in the Soviet "film grading" procedures described earlier, the PLAAF's was even worse. Indeed, one Chinese aviation historian admitted that during the last year of the war "as more and more MiGs were lost, the pressure on units and pilots to exact revenge mounted, and the tendency for exaggeration became inevitable". Consequently, official "victory credits" also cannot be used to tally enemy aircraft destroyed.

In fact, the only relatively reliable method is to research the air arms' logistics accounts where unit losses incurred are documented. Even these, if political pressures influence their accounting, can be flawed, but because of the logistician's responsibility to account for issued equipment they will be relatively accurate. While recently released official Soviet and Chinese histories now provide a reliably objective view into the Communist MiG-15 losses, the often fragmentary and conveniently inaccurate causal determinations in official USAF aircraft loss records provide the historian with

immense work researching each aircraft written off to determine if it should be more correctly attributed to enemy fighter action.

A thorough, individual review of USAF Korean War F-86 loss records results in the determination that 224 Fifth Air Force Sabres were lost during the conflict. Forty-seven pilots were killed, 65 listed as missing and 26 captured, with another six wounded but able to return to friendly control. Of the 224 F-86s lost, 40 were in non-operational accidents, 61 to non-enemy causes during operational sorties, 18 to AAA and one to an enemy bombing (night Po-2) attack. This leaves a maximum of 104 lost as a result of aerial combat. Seventy-eight of these are known to have been due directly to action by MiG-15s, with another 14 caused by fuel starvation as a result of combat or battle damage, bringing the total number of Sabres lost during combat with MiGs to 92. The remaining 12 failed to return from their missions, and with their losses not observed and the pilots listed as MIA, the cause of their demise is unknown.

Soviet archival records state that 335 MiG-15s and 120 pilots were lost in Korea, with 319 of these aircraft and 110 pilots being shot down in combat. All but ten of the downed MiGs fell to F-86s. The PLAAF admits the loss of 399 aircraft in Korea, of which 224 MiG-15s were destroyed in combat – all exclusively by the Sabre – with the loss of 77 pilots. North Korean losses are not yet known with certainty, but in 1953 a defector estimated that KPAF MiG losses numbered at least 100 jets, of which about one-third had been claimed by F-86s. Overall then, during the course of the conflict approximately 566 MiG-15s had been destroyed by Sabres. Of all these, only 49 were flown by members of the two elite V-VS divisions that fought over the Yalu primarily during 1951. The remaining 517 MiG-15s were lost by PVO, PLAAF and KPAF units in the 18 months from February 1952 until the ceasefire went into effect on July 27, 1953.

Accepting USAF losses as described above, this generates an overall "kill ratio" of 5.835 MiG-15s destroyed for each Sabre lost. However, against the Soviet's best – the crack 303rd and 324th IADs – the ratio nears parity at 1.4-to-1. Interestingly, when the 324th IAD was flying the early model MiG, the "kill ratio" was 8-to-1 in favour of the F-86A. Once the MiG-15bis was used, it dropped to 1.2-to-1, indicating that the two variants, and the men flying them, were nearly equal in capabilities. The aerial battles of 1951 in terms of "kill ratio" alone were essentially a draw. But against the other Soviet, Chinese and Korean MiG divisions, the F-86A/E/F reigned supreme with a "kill ratio" of 9.07-to-1.

The obvious conclusion is that while the F-86A/E and MiG-15bis were probably equally matched, the F-model Sabres flown by well-trained and experienced American (and British and Canadian exchange) fighter pilots were far superior to their inadequately trained and marginally experienced adversaries flying an increasingly outdated jet fighter.

The Korean War ceasefire saw the sun set on the MiG-15. Having performed respectably in the hands of the Soviets' best pilots, it was already being eclipsed by the newer, higher performance MiG-17, which entered V-VS service in October 1952 – well before the war had ended. (FoxbatFiles.com)

While the overall ratio of 5.8-to-1 does not meet the USAF's Korean War mythology of a 10-to-1 "kill ratio", it stands as one of the highest in the history of aerial combat.

Finally, this discussion should end where it began – "kill claims". USAF F-86 pilots claimed 800 MiG-15s destroyed when "only" 566 were lost. This results in an overestimation – based largely on gun camera film recording of hits, but the target surviving to RTB – of 29.25 per cent.

Although Soviet V-VS units had stringent "kill claim" criteria on paper, of which their flawed "film grading" procedure was the central basis, it was rarely assiduously applied. For example, not only would victories sometimes be credited based on film alone (even if the pilot did not claim a kill), GCI reporting that the target had disappeared from their radar scope was considered adequate confirmation, when actually the target had descended beneath the radar coverage and escaped. During the first 16 months of combat Soviet V-VS units claimed 218 F-86s destroyed when only 36 (35 to the two elite IADs and one to the 50th IAD) had been lost. This results in a 600 per cent inflation rate in victory credits over actual Sabres destroyed!

The follow-on Soviet units claimed an additional 429 F-86s destroyed, and the PLAAF (which had even less stringent criteria applied less rigorously) credited its divisions with 211 Sabres destroyed, for a total of 640 F-86s claimed destroyed when 62 were actually lost – an exaggeration of over 1,000 per cent! Outrageously, the North Koreans claimed to have destroyed 5,729 UNC aircraft, but do not specify how many of this astronomical figure were supposedly F-86s.

Clearly, unit "kill claims" and official "victory credits" cannot be used to determine who won the battle for aerial superiority in "MiG Alley".

AFTERMATH

The two-and-a-half-year contest between the MiG-15 and F-86 over the Yalu was the struggle for aerial superiority over the rear areas of the Communist military forces in Korea. Air superiority is achieved, defensively, if the enemy is denied the ability to conduct aerial operations without incurring disruption, hindrance or prohibitive loss. Offensively, of course, it is achieved when air superiority fighters enable friendly air operations to consistently strike their objectives without interference from enemy air forces. Because the USAF persisted in using slow, vulnerable and obsolete B-29s in its bombing campaigns, these proved impossible for the fast, modern F-86s to protect, and the Sabres failed to establish a permissive environment in which the Superfortresses could conduct their operations unimpeded. Against the MiG-15, the F-86 could not achieve air superiority for them.

The MiG-15bis led directly to the MiG-17, which incorporated increased (45° inner/42° outer) wing sweep, a longer, more streamlined empennage and an afterburning VK-1F turbojet engine. The MiG-17 retained its predecessor's excellent maneuverability, making it a worthy and effective adversary for USAF F-105s and F-4 Phantom IIs over North Vietnam 12 years later. (Tim Callaway Collection)

After October 1951 it was fighter-bombers that carried the UNC's aerial campaign to the enemy, and for the rest of the war there were no F-80C or F-84E fighter-bomber strikes against any target in North Korea disrupted or defeated by MiG-15s. In fact, in the single most dramatic and strategically important mission of the war – the Supung hydro-electric powerplant strike in June 1952 – the Communists did not even attempt to challenge the Sabre's dominance of "MiG Alley". And this was not, as most MiG apologists assert, due to weather preventing them from launching sorties from the Andong complex bases.

This event provided moot testimony to the Sabre finally achieving air superiority within this hotly contested arena. From that mission on – with the Soviet MiG forces gradually being withdrawn from the confrontation (defined by declining daily average sortie counts) and the PLAAF experiencing increasingly "appalling" losses – the USAF air dominance, provided by the F-86F, was assured.

The conclusion, therefore, is that the MiG-15bis, when flown by the well trained and combat experienced veterans of the two elite V-VS fighter divisions, was able to hold its own against the similarly piloted USAF Sabre. The significance of effective training and combat experience is illustrated by the fact that of the 22 HSUs awarded to Soviet airmen for their exploits in the Korean conflict, 18 went to members of these IADs, while the other four were awarded to men flying during the last 18 months of combat (and one of these was a nightfighter pilot).

The most significant legacy provided by the USAF's F-86s in Korea was the cadre of combat-experienced instructors who institutionalized air-to-air fighter training for subsequent generations of American fighter pilots. Teaching at Nellis's "Fighter School" in the mid-1950s were (left to right, standing) Capt R. H. Moore (5 kills), Capt Bob Latshaw (5 kills), Maj William Whisner (5.5 kills) and Capt Iven Kincheloe (6 kills), and (kneeling) Lt Col George Jones (6.5 kills). (John Henderson via Warren Thompson)

The overall assessment then has to be that the MiG-15bis and F-86A/E/F were nearly equally matched fighters, and the difference, made much more apparent in later months, was provided by the training, experience and morale of the men flying them.

From their perspective, aircraft designers on both sides drew conclusions that drove subsequent fighter designs. Seeking increased performance to beat the F-86F, Soviet designers developed the MiG-15bis45 – quickly redesignated the MiG-17 – which had increased wing sweepback, a longer/finer fuselage and an afterburning VK-1F engine. The next iteration – the MiG-19 – increased wing sweepback even more, to 55 degrees, and incorporated two afterburning turbojets to become the Soviets' first truly transonic fighter.

Similarly, American designers also pushed for increased performance, the NAA F-100 Super Sabre achieving this, as well as solving the F-86's greatest deficiency by mounting four 20mm cannon for its armament. Legendary Lockheed designer Clarence "Kelly" Johnson took the quest for superior performance to the extreme with the high altitude, supersonic F-104 Starfighter. However, both these designs lost sight of the fighter pilot's need for maneuverability and both were thrashed by the follow-on MiG-21 over the Taiwan Straits and Vietnam.

In fact, for the USAF, the greatest legacy of the "MiG Alley" experience was not in equipment but in the tactics learned and taught by combat-experienced Sabre pilots. These became the basis during the next decade for the USAF's air superiority campaign over North Vietnam, even when hamstrung with inappropriate equipment (the missile-only F-4 Phantom II bomber interceptor and fleet defender) and constrained by oppressive political restrictions. To achieve the prerequisite of air superiority, the USAF was finally able to make its civilian masters realize that a modern jet fighter had to have excellent maneuverability as well as unparalleled performance – hence the creation of the F-15 Eagle. But despite its awesome capabilities the men and women flying the Eagle still had to diligently apply the tactical lessons learned by their Sabre-flying forebears in the unforgiving aerial arena known to us as "MiG Alley".

FURTHER READING

The full story of what happened in "MiG Alley" in the early 1950s is, naturally, not to be gleaned from any single source. Because of the obsessively secretive nature of the Communist side of the conflict, Western aviation historians have had to rely on USAF records and personal accounts. This has resulted in several excellent, though largely "one sided", histories by notable authors such as Korean War expert Robert F. Dorr and Sabre guru Larry Davis. More recently John R. Bruning has produced a good popular history called *Crimson Sky – The Air Battle for Korea* (Brassey's, 1999). More authoritative is Kenneth P. Werrell's *Sabres over MiG Alley* (Naval Institute Press, 2005), but this otherwise outstanding account labors under the false assumption that "kill claims" equate to numbers of enemy aircraft actually destroyed.

Since the mid-1990s the Russian government has released vaults of Soviet Cold War archival documents, many of which have been translated by the Woodrow Wilson International Center for Scholars, most notably by Dr. Kathryn Weathersby, and the accounts of Korean War veterans have proliferated in Russian press and book publications. For example, the experiences of Sergei Kramarenko were translated from his memoir *Protiv Messerov i Seybrov – V Nebe Dbukh Voyn* ("Against Messerschmitts and Sabres – In the Sky of Two Wars"), which was also recently produced in English as *Air Combat Over the Eastern Front & Korea* (Pen & Sword, 2008).

Korean War analyst Stephen Sewell has done Western historians a great service with his prolific translation of pre-eminent Russian publications (titles translated) such as the official *The War in Korea 1950-1953* (St Petersburg, Izdatel'stvo Poligon, 2000) edited by N. L. Volkovskiu, and *Russia (USSR) in Local Wars and Regional Conflicts in the Second Half of the 20th Century* (Moscow, Kuchkov Polye, 2000) edited by Maj Gen V. A. Zolotarev. Additionally, Sewell's translation of Vitaliy Naboka's *NATO's Hawks in the Sights of Stalin's Falcons – Soviet Flyers in the Protection of the Skies of*

China and Korea (1950-1951) (Sovietskaya Kuban Publishing, 1999) supplies a rich source of information on the first year of this aerial contest. Anatoliy Demin's "In the Skies of Korea – The 'Eagles' of Mao Zedong Against the 'Hawks' of Uncle Sam" series published in *Mir Aviatsii* ("World Aviation") relates the Soviet view of PLAAF involvement in the Korean War while Vladislav Morozov and Sergey Uskov's "On Guard for Peace and Labor – The KPRK Air Forces from 1948 to 1998" (also published in *Mir Aviatsii*) covers the KPAF performance from the Soviet perspective.

Dr. Xiaoming Zhang, a second generation Chinese-American and currently a professor at the USAF Air War College, was granted access to the PRC's governmental archives and allowed to interview PLAAF Korean War veterans. From his research he has produced the definitive study (in English, anyway) of the PLAAF's involvement in the Korean War, covering the subject at every level, from national leadership aims and decisions down to individual fighter pilot tactics and actions. His book, *Red Wings Over the Yalu – China, the Soviet Union and the Air War in Korea*, is a must-read on this subject.

Finally, North Korean defector No Kum-Sok's memoir *A MiG-15 to Freedom* rounds out the coverage from the Communist side of the conflict, providing excellent details on the organization and actions of the KPAF, as well as personal accounts of what it was like for a young, inexperienced Korean MiG-15 pilot to face battle-hardened American Sabre pilots over his home country.

For the serious students of this subject, all of the above are recommended.

In addition to those mentioned, other sources used in this account are:

BOOKS AND MAGAZINES

Blesse, Frederick C., *No Guts, No Glory!* (HQ Tactical Air Command, 1955)

Curtis, Duncan, *North American F-86 Sabre* (The Crowood Press Ltd, 2000)

Davis, Larry, *The 4th Fighter Wing in the Korean War* (Schiffer Publishing Ltd, 2001)

Dorr, Robert F., *Osprey Combat Aircraft 42 – B-29 Superfortress Units of the Korean War* (Osprey Publishing Limited, 2003)

Futrell, Robert Frank, *The United States Air Force in Korea, 1950-1953* (Office of Air Force History, 1981)

Gordon, Yefim and Vladimir Rigmant, *MiG-15 – Design, Development and Korean War Combat History* (Motorbooks International Publishers, 1993)

Krylov, Leonid and Yuriy Tepsurkaev, *Osprey Aircraft of the Aces 82 – Soviet MiG-15 Aces of the Korean War* (Osprey Publishing Limited, 2008)

McGill, Earl J., *Black Tuesday over Namsi – The True History of the Epic Air Battle of the Korean War* (Heritage Books, Inc, 2008)

Thompson, Warren E. and David R. McLaren, *MiG Alley – Sabres vs MiGs Over Korea* (Specialty Press, 2002)

Wildenberg, Thomas, "The A-1C(M) Gunsight – A Case Study of Technological Innovation in the United States Air Force", *Air Power History*, Vol. 36, No. 2, pp. 28-37

INDEX

References to illustrations are shown in **bold**.